TOURING IN WINE COUNTRY
PROVENCE

MITCHELL BEAZLEY

TOURING IN WINE COUNTRY
PROVENCE

HUBRECHT DUIJKER

SERIES EDITOR
HUGH JOHNSON

Contents

Dedication
*For my hospitable Provençal-Dutch friends,
Tineke and Eugène*

**Touring in Wine Country
Provence**
By Hubrecht Duijker

First published in Great Britain in 1998
by Mitchell Beazley, an imprint of
Octopus Publishing Limited, 2-4 heron
Quays, London, E14 4JP

Revised editions 2001

Copyright © Octopus Publishing Limited
1998, 2001
Text copyright © Hubrecht Duijker
1998, 2001
Maps copyright © Octopus Publishing
Limited 1998, 2001

ISBN 1 84000 046 5

A CIP catalogue record of this book is
available from the British Library

Commissioning Editor: Sue Jamieson
Executive Art Editor: Fiona Knowles
Senior Editor: Roz Cooper
Senior Art Editor: Wayne Blades
Design: Watermark Communications
Cartographic Editor: Zoë Goodwin
Picture Research: Claire Gouldstone
Index/Gazetteer: Ann Barrett
Production: Rachel Lynch
Cartography: Colin Earl Cartography

Typeset in Bembo and Gill Sans
Printed and bound by Toppan Printing
Company Limited, China

Foreword

Hubrecht Duijker clocks up the mileage of a road haulier in his peregrinations back and forth across the wine countries of Europe. If anyone knows France (viticultural France, at least) like the back of his hand, it is Hubrecht.

With his first ground-breaking book on the less-famous chateaux of Bordeaux, he invented a genre: the personal, in-depth investigation of wine-growers, their wines, families, homes and tastes – all illustrated with his excellent photographs. In our *Wine Touring Guides*, he reorganises his thoughts and experiences to lead wine-tourists on the routes he knows so well: to his favourite producers, favourite hotels and restaurants, and to the sights, landscapes, markets and monuments that give the visitor the truest feel of each region.

There are a host of reasons for visiting Provence: its climate, its landscapes and seascapes, its ancient monuments, rustic food, general *douceur de vivre* and the real or imagined simplicity of its people. But few, I expect, visit Provence primarily for the sake of its wine. It is more a question of wanting to know what is best to drink after having arrived. Traditionally, it was a question asked after the tenth bottle of indifferent and over-strong rosé in a tone of desperation, but happily, in recent years, the influx of more demanding visitors – and more importantly, the wave of wealthy settlers, permanent or part-time, in its beautiful old *bastides* – has brought a massive quality change.

Provence is not entirely without its names of old renown. However, only one – Bandol – has a modern reputation as a wine of international significance. Bandol is the unique product of an awkward grape, Mourvèdre, but at its best, it is one of the most forthright and soul-stirring of French reds. Even so, most Provençal wines of quality are introductions, the result of treating this ancient landscape as a 'New World' vineyard. The best wines of today are made by marrying the traditional grape varieties of the region (none of them superstars by any standard) with the international favourites – above all Cabernet Sauvignon and Syrah.

Red wines are the strong suit of modern Provence. Rosés (still in the majority) are emerging as potentially fresh, vivid and fruity, or at least mild and disarming. Whites are still struggling, with few exceptions. On the coast near Marseille Cassis is a famous name with sturdy, unexceptional whites. But the curious thing about Provence, for all its torrid summers, is that red wines (and up to a point, rosés) are what go down best with the positive, strongly accented cuisine.

Provence is a wide and diffuse area – harder to define than you might think. From the Rhône Valley to the point where the Alps Maritimes make their final plunge into the sea (just east of Menton; indeed the Italian border) lies a stretch of forest and mountains which is magic for holidays, but tough to cultivate.

Hubrecht's guide offers a new way of exploring this haunting, pine-scented country – but in a way which, in a few year's time, will seem as natural a circuit of the Rhône, Alsace, or any one of France's wonderfully various wine regions.

Hugh Johnson

Introduction

Provence as an historical entity was created by the Romans who regarded it as a 'province' of their empire. From an administrative point of view, the region has, since 1790, consisted of five *départements*: Alpes de Haute-Provence, Alpes-Maritimes, Bouches-du-Rhône, Var and Vaucluse.

However, the wine region of Provence itself is smaller than this because a large part of the Vaucluse is included in the wine region of the Rhône. The only part of the Vaucluse covered by this guide is Côtes du Lubéron. The majority of Provence's vineyards are in the *département* of the Var; the vineyards in the Alpes de Haute-Provence and Alpes-Maritimes amount to less than 400 hectares together.

This guide describes just those parts of Provence where the wine is produced. Together they cover an enormous area. At the western extremity are the vineyards situated near Les Baux-de-Provence in the Rhône delta, while the furthest east are the vineyards of the Bellet *appellation* in the hills behind Nice. The most northerly point is Apt, at the foot of the Montagne du Lubéron, while the vineyards on the breathtakingly beautiful Ile de Porquerolles represent the southernmost point.

AN IDEAL CLIMATE

Since the Second World War Provence has become an increasingly popular holiday destination. One of the reasons is its pleasant, mild and sunny climate. Provence boasts between 2,700 and 2,800 hours of sunshine in a year; this is much more than Paris with its 1,800 hours of sun, and almost twice the number of hours enjoyed in London and other north European cities. The average temperature in summer is around 22°C, while in January and the other winter months it is about 8°C. The temperatures become more extreme the further inland you go and the higher the

Left *Blossom time at Domaine Richeaume, AOC Côtes de Provence, an organic wine estate.*

Above *Rich sunset colours and picturesque old mills have inspired many an artist in Provence.*

Provence

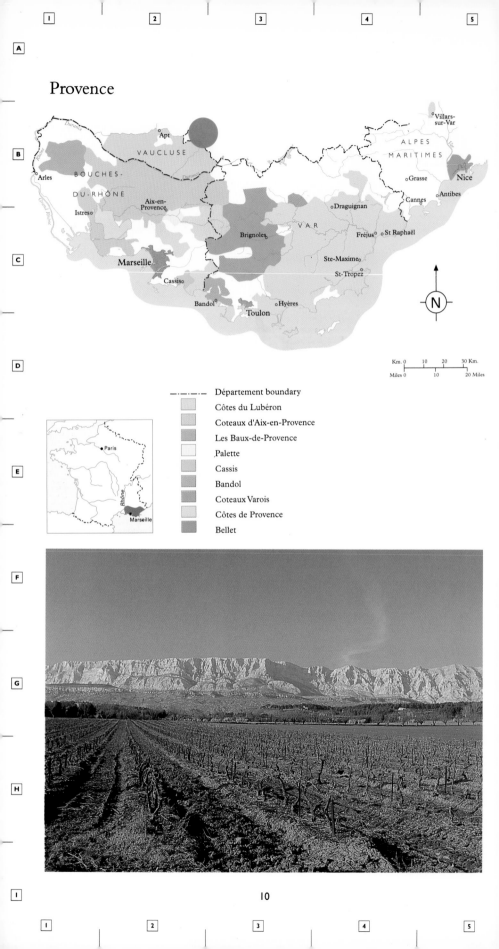

Km. 0   10   20   30 Km.

Miles 0   10   20 Miles

----·----· Département boundary

Côtes du Lubéron

Coteaux d'Aix-en-Provence

Les Baux-de-Provence

Palette

Cassis

Bandol

Coteaux Varois

Côtes de Provence

Bellet

Above *Luminous purple fields of lavender flowers, destined to be distilled down to use as essence for the perfume industry based around the town of Grasse.*

altitude. Rainfall occurs mainly in late autumn and early spring, while the *mistral,* the strong local wind which comes from the Alps, blows here all too frequently, although less than it does in the Rhône Valley. This wind does, however, have the advantage of ensuring that the vine stocks remain free of disease and do not rot.

A LANDSCAPE OF CONTRASTS
Nature in Provence is like a magnet, attracting millions of tourists from the more northern parts of Europe and farther afield. Its amazing beauty overwhelms visitors who are always fascinated by its variety and contrasts. Along the coastline of the Côte d'Azur are long sandy beaches alternating with rocky cliffs, spectacular bays and charming inlets. The interior is dominated by a series of mountain ranges; from west to east, Les Alpilles, Montagne du Lubéron, Montagne Ste-Victoire, the Massif de la Ste-Baume, and the Massif des Maures. You are always surrounded by hills in Provence, either close by or on the horizon. These hills are often covered with dense woodland and shrubs or cut by deep gorges. The most famous of these ravines is the Gorges du Verdon in the most northern part

Left *The sculptural Montagne Ste-Victoire, seen from afar, often painted by the artist Paul Cézanne.*

of the Var, but they can also be found in other places such as Ollioules (Bandol), slightly to the north of Draguignan, and near Bellet (Gorges de la Vésubie).

Above *Spectacular mountain backdrop for Mas de la Dame, the largest estate in the quality Les Baux-de-Provence red wine area.*

The mountain ranges are interspersed with low hills and fertile valleys, rivers and streams, adding up to one of the most glorious areas for landscape in all of France.

FLOWERS AND FRUIT

The vegetation of Provence is luxuriant. Shrubs, conifers, cypresses, palms, oaks and chestnut trees all flourish and there are flowers in abundance. Everywhere, flowers are evident in gardens, on balconies or simply growing wild. The village of Bormes-les-Mimosas is even named after a flower, while the town of Ollioules boasts the largest flower auction in France.

Since the 19th century, cut flowers have been cultivated more in the *département* of the Var than anywhere else in France. Nice is another centre for growing cut flowers, especially carnations, and a wide range of other plants. In the Var alone some 45 varieties of roses are available as well as 35 different mimosas. Provence also produces enormous quantities of lavender. This means that a visit in high summer brings scent from fragrant purple fields of lavender, destined to become essence for the perfume centres in Grasse, and also a magnet for the honey bee.

Fruit, including of course the grape from which wine is made, and the olive, is widely cultivated in Provence. There are still many working mills where olive oil is produced and Mouriès, in the wine region of Les Baux, is France's largest olive-producing *commune*. The Massif des Maures is famous for the great quantities of chestnuts it produces and for many generations the main income in villages such as La Garde-Freinet has come from their cultivation. A *Fête de la Châtaigne* (chestnut festival) is still celebrated in several villages in the Massif des Maures on Sundays between

Right *Cotignac village; perched romantically against a cliff face, with its fine ruined castle.*

12

October and the end of November. And walking in the wild you cannot fail to enjoy the delicious fragrance of the famous Provençal herbs: basil, rosemary and thyme.

AN ENVIABLE LIFESTYLE

Another attractive aspect of Provence is its relaxed lifestyle. In the early evening when the worst of the heat is over, people meet in the village square in the shade of the plane trees to enjoy a glass of wine. The game of *pétanque* or *boules* is played very seriously throughout the day. The rules are simple: there are two teams and each must try to get its *boules* (steel balls) as close as possible to a smaller one, the jack or *cochonnet*. The game was probably invented in Le Ciotat (between Cassis and Bandol) in 1907, where there is even an Avenue de la Pétanque. If the game is played over a distance of more than ten metres, it is called *longue*.

You can sample every kind of sport in Provence, including swimming, diving, canoeing, rock climbing, tennis, sailing, flying, car racing and golf, a sport which is becoming increasingly popular.

A SOURCE OF INSPIRATION

The truly idyllic nature of Provence has inspired many artists who have immortalised its beauty in their paintings. Van Gogh painted near St-Rémy-de-Provence, Cézanne was fascinated by the Montagne Ste-Victoire, while painters such as Bonnard, Braque, Chagall, Van Dongen, Dufy, Kandinsky, Matisse, Monet, Picasso and Renoir found their inspiration in the beauty of the coast between St-Tropez and Nice. The architecture in Provence is as varied as the landscape. One is conscious of an Italian influence in many villages and monuments which is explained partly by the close proximity to Italy, and also by the fact that Italian

Above *The traditional blue and yellow tones of Provençal textile design, here in Cadenet, Lubéron.*

Top right *The Gorges du Verdon is Europe's widest and deepest gorge; not to be missed.*

families were invited to come and settle in Provence to repopulate and rebuild the villages (such as Bagnols-en-Forêt, near Fréjus).

In the 15th century, *le bon roi René* ('good king René') encouraged many Italian artists to come and work in the land he ruled. As a result, Gothic churches are quite rare in Provence (the one at St-Maximin-la-Ste-Baume is the most impressive), while fine Romanesque churches abound. There are also some magnificent abbeys to be visited, such as Le Thoronet, which was built in a typical Cistercian style.

TOURISM

Unfortunately, Provence's idyllic character is now being threatened by the enormous influx of tourists. The coast can be extremely busy during summer; around St-Tropez it may be easier to move by ferry than boat from harbour to harbour. However, during the 1990s a new consciousness has arisen about environmental issues and *départements* such as the Var have taken measures to safeguard areas of natural beauty. As well, subsidies have been granted for the upkeep and restoration of houses built in the original Provençal style.

Fortunately, most vineyards are inland, away from the busy coastal region. This guide will help you discover the wine villages where you will be able to enjoy tranquillity in an authentic Provençal atmosphere.

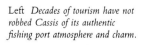

Left *Decades of tourism have not robbed Cassis of its authentic fishing port atmosphere and charm.*

Provence: a look at its history

Provence has been inhabited since antiquity, as is shown by the existence of dolmens, prehistoric monuments estimated to be some 4,500 years old. These can be found in several places in Provence, for example near the towns of Brignoles and Cabasse.

In 1000BC Provence was inhabited by the Ligurians. They were followed by the Greeks, who in 594BC founded Massalia, which became Marseille as we know it today. The Greeks came from the town of *Phocaea* (modern Fotcha) in the Asiatic part of Turkey. The Phoceans were a major trading power who founded settlements all along the Mediterranean coast as commercial centres. They then built trading posts near these settlements, including around the port of Massalia.

The Greeks brought vine stocks with them, including Ugni Blanc. They also introduced their winemaking techniques into Provence. The many amphorae discovered along the Provençal coast testify to a lively trade. For instance, as many as 10,000 of these Greek wine containers were found on the Ile de Riou, a little island situated between Marseille and Cassis. Further tangible evidence of the Greek occupation is the ship that was discovered in 1992 when an underground car park was built in Marseille, not far from the Old Port.

Above *The Romanesque chapel of St-Sixte near Eygalières, in the heart of Les Baux-de-Provence.*

THE ROMAN PERIOD

The Greeks were followed by the Celts and then the Romans. It is to the latter that Provence owes its name, the Romans having named the region *Provincia Romana*. Julius Caesar conquered the whole of Gaul between 58 and 51BC. Two years after his victory Julius Caesar built a new harbour for his war fleet, *Colonia Octavanorum Pacensis Classica Forum Julii*, which became the town of Fréjus.

During the period of peaceful Roman rule known as the *Pax Romana*, which would last until the fourth century, Provence enjoyed a time of great prosperity. Winemaking also prospered as an industry, as can be seen from the paintings; mosaics; amphorae and remains of the factories which made them; fermentation vats; and cellars. There are many other traces of Roman civilisation in Provence, ranging from gigantic amphitheatres to the remains of a Gallo–Roman villa in the Domaine du Loou in La Roquebrussanne.

THE SARACENS

The decline of the Roman Empire led to invasions by Barbarian tribes such as the Visigoths, Bugundi, Saxons and Lombards. Around AD700, Provence was threatened by the Saracens, Moorish Arabs from Spain. Not content with

Left *Thousand-year-old stone carvings in the cloisters of the Cathédrale St-Sauveur, Aix-en-Provence.*

17

merely attacking and plundering from the sea, they moved further inland. In 884 they built a fortress at Fraxinet, which was to become La Garde-Freinet. This village is situated in a mountain range which was named after the invaders: the Massif des Maures. Large parts of Provence fell into the hands of the Saracens who built castles and citadels, town walls and fortified town gates all over the region.

In 940, they attacked Fréjus and pillaged the town, killing the inhabitants or taking them into slavery. However, the Moors also brought with them the art of medicine and introduced the tapping of resin from pine trees, the manufacture of tiles and many other things. In 973, the invaders were driven out by William the Liberator, the first Count of Provence.

SPANISH AND FRENCH DYNASTIES

This was the beginning of Provence as a *comté* (earldom). In 1112, a descendant of William the Liberator married Raimond Bérenger, Count of Barcelona. The Spanish House remained in power until 1245 when Provence once again had a French ruler, Charles of Anjou, who in 1246 married his own sister-in-law Beatrice Bérenger.

The last Count of Provence was René of Anjou, known as *le bon roi René*. He ruled from 1436 to 1480, bringing great prosperity to the region. He encouraged winemaking and introduced the Muscat grape; there is a statue of him with a bunch of grapes in the Cours Mirabeau in Aix-en-Provence. On January 15, 1482, René d'Anjou's nephew bequeathed Provence to the French Crown, except for the town of Nice which belonged to the Duke of Savoy, a situation which was to remain unchanged until 1860. The *seigneurie* (domain) of Monaco had already been bought by the Grimaldi family from the Genoese in the tenth century, and they are still the ruling family there today.

Above Dramatic remains of a Roman temple at Château Bas.

Top right A tranquil corner of the 12th-century Cistercian abbey of Le Thoronet, in the heart of the Var.

Right Glanum is a well-preserved Roman settlement near Les Baux, built in the Hellenistic style.

A BATTLEFIELD

Now part of the French crown, the peace of Provence was disrupted in the 16th and 18th centuries by violent Wars of Religion and by the great plague epidemics of 1580 and 1720. In 1746, during the War of Succession, Provence was invaded by an alliance of Austria and Piedmont, supported by the British fleet. The British warships were back in action in 1793, this time in Toulon, to help the royalists in their (unsuccessful) fight against Napoleon's revolutionaries.

Provence was the scene of dramatic events during the Second World War: in 1942, when the French fleet was scuttled in Toulon harbour to prevent it falling into enemy hands, and on August 15, 1944, when airborne divisions were dropped near Le Muy and the first troops landed at La Nartelle. Two weeks later Provence was liberated.

Viticulture
and wines

Provence rightly calls itself the oldest wine-producing region in France because wine has been made here for some 26 centuries, and for most of this time it has been exported. From *Forum Julii* (today called Fréjus) the Romans shipped large quantities of wine to Italy, and in the Middle Ages England also began to import wine from Provence after Henry II of England married Eleanor of Aquitaine. Charles II (in 1292) and Queen Mary (in 1391) also concluded commercial treaties with Provence.

The export of Provençal wine continued to grow as time went by. In the 17th and 18th centuries wine exports had become so important that Provence was the second most-important wine region in France, after Bordeaux. The demand for Provençal wine continued to rise in the 19th century, resulting in a massive expansion of the area of vineyards: between 1800 and 1850 it doubled to 90,000 hectares. This enormous growth was undoubtedly also a reaction to the repeal of Louis XV's edict in 1731 forbidding the planting of new vineyards in Provence. Since antiquity the region has produced light-coloured red wines, forerunners of today's rosés, but during the 19th century robust red wines also became particularly popular, although according to writers of the period, their quality often left much to be desired.

Top right   Neatly pruned, dormant vines set below the AOC Côtes de Provence village of Pourrières.

Right   Wood fermentation vats at Château Romassan in Bandol, one of the Ott family's estates.

A SERIES OF DISASTERS

In the middle of the 19th century the demand for Provençal wine began to decrease. One of the reasons was the arrival of the railways which made it possible to transport enormous quantities of wine rapidly from the Languedoc to Paris. This new competition from the wines of the Languedoc proved fatal for a large number of Provençal winegrowers. The situation was so bad in some years that they did not sell any wine at all and it had to be thrown away to make room for the next year's production. The winemakers' plight was further aggravated in 1851, when their vines were infected by a wilting disease called oidium and 30 years later by mildew. The growers had barely recovered from these problems when Provence was struck by the vine louse *Phylloxera vastatrix*. As elsewhere in France it destroyed almost all the vinestocks in Provence. In the *département* of the Var alone more than 50,000 hectares were destroyed by phylloxera between 1871 and 1891; that is almost two-thirds of the total area of vines, which had already shrunk by 15 per cent since 1850.

RECOVERY AND COOPERATION

The only way to fight phylloxera was to graft French vines onto American root stocks. This costly operation of grafting, lifting and replanting meant that winegrowers had to work as economically as possible. Prior to this problem, vineyards were often located halfway up hillsides, on terraces bordered by olive trees, while fruit orchards, vegetables and corn fields grew in the valley itself. However, to ensure a regular, more easily harvested crop, winegrowers decided to plant their vines at lower levels, as many of their counterparts were doing in the Languedoc. They also switched over to more productive red grape varieties such as the Carignan. The excellent Mourvèdre almost completely disappeared. At the same time the first cooperatives were set up. The earliest was founded in Cotignac in 1905. Four decades later there were nearly 100 in the *département* of the Var, and more than half of them are still in existence today. These *caves coopératives* produce approximately 60 per cent of the Côtes de Provence wines. Some have interesting names such as L'Amicale (in Cuers), La Fraternelle (Pourrières) and La Laborieuse (Carnoules).

SURVIVAL

In the first half of the 20th century the primary aim of the most important appellation, Côtes de Provence, was to survive. Producers tried to make wines of decent quality in large quantities, at as high a price as possible. This is why Côtes de Provence had to wait such a long time before being elevated to the rank of *appellation contrôlée*, and why it only happened in 1977. Smaller Provençal districts with stricter quality standards were granted the status several decades before Côtes de Provence: Cassis in 1936; Bandol and Bellet in 1941; and Palette in 1948. Côtes de Provence also began to produce more rosé wines, which still today represent three-quarters of its production. Only a few winegrowers concentrated on producing quality wines.

Marcel Ott had introduced the Bordeaux grape varieties Cabernet Sauvignon and Sémillon to Provence as long ago as 1896. Some 75 years later, Cabernet Sauvignon was planted at Château Vignelaure with resounding success. Today, both Cabernet Sauvignon and Sémillon are officially recognised in the Côtes de Provence appellation.

CRUS CLASSES

In 1932, four conscientious winegrowers formed an association which aimed to improve the quality of their wine; membership grew and it became a syndicate to campaign for AOC status. The Institut National des Appellations d'Origine Contrôlée sought to help the *domaines* which were members of the syndicate – the better ones who bottled their wine themselves. During the German occupation in the Second World War, the sale of Côtes de Provence was not permitted because the name was not legally recognised. Their solution was to raise the wines in question to the rank of *cru classé* (classed growth) whereby they could be sold under the name Côtes de Provence.

The intention was that the *cru classé* description would simply disappear after the war, but this did not happen. The number of *crus classés* even increased, to 23 in 1955. The legislative powers were not happy with the situation. As a result it was decided that no new *domaines* should be added. Since then the number of estates with *cru classé* status has declined because some of them have ceased to exist, and the present list contains just 18 names:

CRUS CLASSES

Domaine de l'Aumérade	**Château Minuty**
Pierrefeu-du-Var	Gassin
Château de Brégançon	**Château Mireille**
Bormes-les-Mimosas	La Londe-les-Maures
Castel Roubine	**Domaine du Noyer**
Lorgues	Bormes-les-Mimosas
Clos Cibonne	**Domaine de Rimauresq**
Le Pradet	Pignans
Domaine de la Clapière	**Château de St-Martin**
Pierrefeu	Taradeau
Domaine de la Croix	**Château St-Maur**
La Croix Valmer	Cogolin
Château du Galoupet	**Château Ste-Roseline**
La Londe-les-Maures	Les Arcs-en-Provence
Domaine du Jas d'Esclans	**Château de Selle**
La Motte	Taradeau
Château de Mauvanne	**Château Ste-Marguerite**
Les Salins d'Hyères	La Londe-les-Maures

Right *Rose bushes planted at the head of each row of vines give an early warning of vine disease or mould infestation. These immaculately kept vines are in the Coteaux d'Aix-en-Provence.*

Top right *Château Vignelaure at Rians was the site of some of the first experimental plantings of Cabernet Sauvignon – not approved for the local AOC at the time, but today they yield some of the best red wines.*

Because there are no official or unofficial quality standards for *crus classés* the title has very little meaning nowadays. The list includes some excellent *domaines*, but there are other non-classified *domaines* of equal importance, and some estates on the list do not deserve to be singled out in this way. The term *cru classé* is therefore no guarantee of superior quality.

Much more important is the Echantelage stamp awarded by the independent Confrérie des Echanteleurs des Côtes de Provence, founded in 1990. The stamp, a kind of quality control guarantee, is awarded to the best wines tasted annually by this Confrérie.

COTES DE PROVENCE TODAY

That Côtes de Provence has not only survived but flourished as a wine region is largely due to its highly successful rosé wines. Rosé wine can be made from a large number of different grape varieties. The main varieties seen here are Carignan (up to a maximum 40 per cent in a blend), Cinsaut, Grenache, Mourvèdre and the unusual Tibouren, a red grape with Greek origins. Besides the primary grape varieties allowed for rosé, there are also a number of permitted secondary varieties, among them Cabernet Sauvignon.

Rosé wines still play a vital part in the Provençal winegrowing industry. This is why growers are continuing to work hard on improving the overall quality of these wines. For instance, the Centre de Recherches du Rosé was set up in Vidauban where a wide range of experiments is taking place. Meanwhile, the Comité Interprofessionnel de Côtes de Provence concentrates its efforts on improving red wines. It organises advisory lectures, makes its own experts available to supervise the production of wine and also has various experimental vineyards, for instance the Domaine de la Bernarde in Le Luc.

As a result of this effort, the quality of the red Côtes de Provence has improved spectacularly since the 1980s. The grape varieties used are almost identical to those used in rosé wines, although secondary varieties such as Cabernet Sauvignon and Syrah are used a lot more and the Tibouren hardly at all. Production of white Côtes de Provence (only five per cent of the production) has also increased considerably: Clairette, Rolle, Sémillon and Ugni Blanc are the permitted grape varieties.

GREAT VARIETY

With an area covering 83 *communes* (parishes) distributed across three *départements* (mainly the Var), and over 50 cooperatives, 350 *domaines* and some 50 wine merchants, Côtes de Provence is certainly the dominant wine region in Provence but not by any means the only one worthy of consideration. Indeed, anyone visiting this region will come across many other Provençal wines, many excellent, from the various other areas described in the course of the book.

Grape varieties

WHITE VARIETIES

Ugni Blanc, or Trebbiano

A real workhorse grape variety that is planted worldwide under various guises. In Provence it is the basis for the majority of white wines, be they Côtes de Provence, Coteaux Varois or Côtes du Lubéron, and yields a fairly bland style of wine, lacking in distinctive varietal character. As a result this grape is popular for blends and for distilling into some of the world's most famous spirits such as Cognac and Armagnac. It is a prolific cropper and keeps a good level of acidity in warm climates.

Clairette

Wines made with this grape were once the basis for highly alcoholic table wine or even vermouth. Clairette thrives in the hot sun of Provence and reaches formidable strength in fermentation. Modern-day taste has veered away from this style and plantings have fallen to match but at its best (at Château Simone (*see* page 56) or in the wines of Cassis (*see* page 101) it can be a rich-flavoured and lingering pleasure.

Roussanne

A grape type famed for inclusion in the fine wines of the Rhône Valley, such as white Hermitage, farther south in Provence it benefits from late ripening to retain good acidity and make powerful, long-lived wines. Its flavour has been compared to that of fine olive oil, quite appropriate in a Provençal context where vines grow alongside olive groves. Apart from straightforward white wines, Roussanne may also be used in blends for rosé or even reds.

Sauvignon Blanc

Famed for its association with the fine white wines of Bordeaux and the Loire, Sauvignon Blanc is a fairly recent phenomenon in the vineyards of Provence and is used to lighten the richness of more traditional varieties with its characteristic 'green' flavours.

Sémillon

Twinned with Sauvignon Blanc in quality Bordeaux white wines, Sémillon grown in Provence yields a vanilla-scented riper style which adds character to blended wines based on the Ugni Blanc grape.

Rolle

An esoteric variety which is exclusive to the small Bellet appellation in the hills behind Nice. As in many of the wines produced in this region, tasters claim they are able to detect salty, herbal aromas in wines made with Rolle; perhaps hints of the rosemary and thyme which grow on the slopes nearby.

Right Roussanne, a grape with distinctive character and style, making wines with potential for keeping.

Below Ugni Blanc, known as St Emilion in the Cognac region, and Trebbiano in Italy.

Below right Grenache is a reliable grape much used in the making of typical Provençal rosé.

RED VARIETIES

Carignan

Much depends on the location of the vineyard for the success of this grape type; on a sunbaked plain it is dull and overripe, but wines from hillside vines are often far better. Like the white Trebbiano grape, this is a workhorse variety grown worldwide on a grand scale. The grapes are thick skinned and late ripening, both advantages in the baking Mediterranean heat of Provence. Carignan is frequently blended with Grenache and Cinsaut to balance its heavy, tannic qualities with fruit. Extra flavour can be extracted by using the fashionable process of carbonic maceration which has the effect of speeding the fermentation and preserving the freshness of the grape. It is widely used for rosé wines.

Grenache

Like Carignan, this grape performs at its best in a blend and it is frequently used for rosé, giving a characteristic orangey tint to the wine and distinguishing it from the Gamay based rosés of the Loire Valley. It is a heavy-yielding variety, and widely planted all over Provence, giving a pleasant fruity quality to many red wines and balancing more pungent flavours such as that of Syrah. One reason for its popularity in making rosé is its relatively thin skin which only lightly tints the wine during fermentation. Most vineyards for Provençal rosé were traditionally sited on flat, sandy plains; the best Grenache wines come from hillside vines which have been able to develop better skins and colour.

Cinsaut

Here is a vine that is ideally adapted to prevailing growing conditions. It thrives on intense heat and arid soils with no reduction in yield and is therefore popular with the *vigneron*; another bonus is that it is tough skinned and rarely damaged by machine harvesting. The downside of its character is revealed in the wines: Cinsaut is said to have a meaty, raw flavour and to be almost unpleasant unless blended. Its heaviness adds weight to rosé and red wines.

Syrah

The great grape of the Rhône Valley is less exciting here but still preserves its characteristic peppery flavour in red wine blends, and is called the *cépage améliorateur* (improver) because it upgrades quite ordinary Provençal wines. Adding Syrah gives a wine the potential to keep and it is particularly agreeable when aged in wood for a year or two.

Cabernet Sauvignon

Marcel Ott (*see* page 22) is credited with the introduction of this noble variety to Provence, and most importantly,

Above Syrah, an aristocratic variety which brings a classy peppery quality to Provençal blends.

Left The fine red wines of the Palette AOC rest their reputation on the Mourvèdre grape, seen here at the premier estate Château Simone.

Right The Rolle grape yields herby, pungent white wine in the tiny Bellet area on the hills behind Nice.

gaining official recognition for it within appellation regulations. It is of course the great grape of Bordeaux and is not a difficult variety to cultivate; as a result it is grown all over the wine world and is successful in most conditions. Provence is far hotter than the Médoc yet the classy Cabernet flavour survives the high temperatures and the resulting red wines are acknowledged as some of the finest from this region. As in the Gironde, the vines do best when grown on a hillside, notably around Aix-en-Provence and especially in Les Baux-de-Provence.

Mourvèdre
A traditional grape for this area and still showing its staying power although it is not a 'noble' variety. Mourvèdre is associated with the best wines of Bandol and definitely adds class to duller grapes such as Cinsaut and Carignan in a blend. Wines made with this grape are said to taste of blackberries.

Fuelle Noir
A survivor of old Provence, still grown above Nice and incorporated into the wines of Bellet, a minute appellation. In style it is powerful but unsubtle, with a rich colour. Another grape variety which may also be used for Bellet wines is the Braquet.

Tibouren
Another native of Provence, which often displays the herbal, almost medicinal qualities of older wine styles. Today it is being planted again to add body and interest to dull rosé wines, but unfortunately it has a tendency to succumb to vine disease.

Vins de Pays

Wine sold as *vin de pays* is often excellent value for money. This appellation, literally meaning 'country wine', was created in the mid-1970s to encourage quality in minor regions, and for the use of growers who wished to experiment with new grape varieties not permitted under the existing *appellation contrôlée* or *vin délimité de qualité supérieure* rules and regulations.

Within Provence, there are various names to look for. Some of them are regional and may be used over an entire *département*; others cover a small zone and may be wines made by a single cooperative. The wines are tested for quality and must conform to various minimum standards for acidity, alcohol levels and yield from each vine grown. The producers' reward is a slightly higher price than they would receive for everyday *vin de table*, and increased kudos in the marketplace.

DEPARTMENTAL VINS DE PAYS
Vin de Pays des Alpes-de-Haute-Provence
Red and rosé wines from the Durance Valley; plus a small amount of white wine, all made with traditional varieties.

Vin de Pays des Bouches-du-Rhône
Covers an extensive area including Aix-en-Provence, the eastern Côtes de Provence section, and the vines grown in the Camargue near Marseille, close to the sea. The majority of the wine is red and may include some Cabernet Sauvignon in the blend.

Vin de Pays du Var
This is country wine from the heartland of Provence; the Var stretches from the mountains around Draguignan to the coast. Rosé accounts for about half of the production, using traditional varieties such as Carignan and Grenache. Do not confuse them with the superior wines sold as Côtes de Provence, but sometimes these wines can be excellent, as is proven by, for example, Domaine de Triennes. Red wines are also made under this appellation but the white wine production is minimal.

Vin de Pays de Vaucluse
A good deal of this area lies in the Rhône Valley and is thus outside the scope of this book. However, *vins de pays* from the Lubéron are included and much of the wine is fairly everyday white made with Ugni Blanc; the red wines are more interesting.

Vin de Pays des Alpes-Maritimes
A range of red, white and rosé wines made in the hills behind Nice and the Riviera coast.

Above *Quaffable, simple Provençal rosé is made from Grenache vines like these near Draguignan.*

Above right *Olive trees and vines are often of equal value to a grower in rural Provence.*

ZONAL VINS DE PAYS
Vin de Pays d'Argens
Wines made around the two valleys of the Issole and Argens in the Var *département;* the majority is rosé but some good red wines are made with Cabernet Sauvignon, and there is small production of white made with traditional grapes such as Clairette and Rolle, as well as the inevitable Ugni Blanc.

Vin de Pays des Maures
These wines come from vineyards in the shadow of the towering Massif des Maures to the west of St-Tropez; they are mainly red and rosé. The total produced is close to a million cases annually.

Vin de Pays du Mont-Caume
Good red wines made in the vicinity of Bandol, plus a few thousand cases of rosé and white.

Vin de Pays de la Petite Crau
As the name implies this is a small area, only including four *communes* in all. Pleasant fruity red wines are made from vines planted in the stony soil around Les Baux-de-Provence. Standards are high and most is vinified by a single cooperative at Noves.

Local cuisine

It is always a pleasure to look around a Provençal market in the spring and summer months. Stalls are overflowing with mouthwatering food, straight from the land or the sea. There are fresh artichokes, aubergines, courgettes, garlic, peppers, all kinds of lettuces, tomatoes, onions and many more types of vegetables. Provence also produces an abundance of fruit such as strawberries, apricots, apples, cherries, melons, pears, peaches and plums.

One of the stalls proffers the most incredible assortment of olives, including those delicious small, black olives from Nice; another sells locally grown herbs and spices of every kind. You will find home-made goats' cheeses, a butcher offering excellent lamb and a fish stall with the most exotic seafood on display such as *rascasse* (scorpion fish), *St-Pierre*, *rouget* (red mullet), anchovies and a variety of other Mediterranean specialities.

Above *Fruit and vegetables thrive in the idyllic climate of Provence; garlic is the essence of local cuisine and artichokes are cooked in a wide variety of styles reflecting both Italian and French influences.*

Left *A market in the old quarter of Nice features a mouthwatering array of olives in their many guises.*

Far left *The area around Les Baux-de-Provence is well known for the olive as well as the vine; France's largest olive oil cooperatives are based here and some olives are sold deliciously flavoured with local herbs.*

LOCAL SPECIALITIES

Because of this wealth of fruit, vegetables, cheese, meat and fish, Provençal cuisine boasts a number of delicious regional dishes. One of the most famous is *tapenade*: the so-called 'caviar of the poor'. This is a paste made from puréed black olives, capers and anchovies; sometimes it includes tuna fish. Black olives are also used in *salade niçoise*, a salad made with tomatoes, green peppers, French beans, anchovies and/or tuna fish, artichoke hearts, onions, olive oil, hard-boiled eggs and of course lettuce. There is in fact no standard recipe for this dish, because everyone has their own interpretation of it. *Pissaladière* is a pizza-like, flat onion tart with black olives and anchovy fillets. Meat dishes are often accompanied by *ratatouille*, a mixture of aubergines, peppers, courgettes, tomatoes and other vegetables, cut into cubes and braised in olive oil and garlic.

FISH SOUP AND GARLIC

The most famous Provençal dish is *bouillabaisse*, a soup which is a meal in itself. It is made from at least three kinds of fish, one of which is invariably *rascasse*. Curnonsky, the famous gastronome, described *bouillabaisse* as the 'golden soup' because of the colour the saffron gives it. The other traditional ingredient is olive oil. *Bouillabaisse* is usually served with *rouille*, a spicy garlic mayonnaise, eaten on toasted bread. Another traditional and equally nourishing fish dish is *bourride*, a fish stew served like soup and made from several kinds of firm, white fish.

Other typically Provençal dishes are *aïoli*, a rich garlic mayonnaise, and *soupe au pistou* which resembles an Italian minestrone: it is a spicy vegetable soup to which finely grated parmesan, ground pine kernels, crushed garlic, basil and olive oil have been added (a mixture called *pesto* in Italy). Provence is also famous for its wide range of delicious fish dishes, such as *filets de rougets au basilic* (fillets of red mullet with basil), which has been one of the specialities of the three-star restaurant L'Oustaù de Baumanière in Les Baux-de-Provence for many years.

MEAT, CHEESE AND FRUIT

Lamb is very popular in Provence. It is prepared in many different ways. *Daube* is a traditional country stew, made with beef. In season game is often on the menu. *Caillettes* are cold meat balls made from minced pork and vegetables (often spinach) and herbs. The cheese platter will include a wide variety of mountain cheeses and goats' cheeses (such as *banon*, wrapped in chestnut leaves). This is followed by pudding, with fruit as the dominant ingredient; in fruit tarts for instance. Dried and candied fruits, such as cherries and apricots, are also typical Provençal specialities.

Top left This fearsome assortment of fish is prized by local gourmets for the flavour it lends to bouillabaisse. Left Sunkissed fruits such as apricots and greengages can be appreciated at their best in this region of France.

Above Freshness is the essence of good sea fish, and there is no shortage of fine quality and choice in the markets of Provence.

How to use this guide

The words and pictures of this book will guide you through the whole of the Provence wine region. The journey starts at Les Baux (between Marseille and Arles) and finishes in the hills near Nice. The order of the chapters is from west to east; the coastal region is dealt with separately for practical reasons. Every chapter describes an itinerary that will guide you through that particular region and the author has personally selected and driven along all these routes himself. They will take you through the most picturesque winegrowing villages and the most beautiful places, as well as giving you addresses and details of the best wine producers.

Every village is described, and interesting historical features and areas of natural beauty are noted. Additional useful information, such as market days, is given wherever possible. The recommended hotels and restaurants include details of the type of accommodation or regional specialities they offer. A number of these places have been recommended by the locals themselves and are rarely or never mentioned in other guidebooks. The winegrowers listed have been selected on a strictly qualitative basis. The list also indicates which type(s) of wine the *domaine* or cooperative produces.

HOTELS

When booking a room, always mention that you want a quiet room, at the back or overlooking a courtyard if there is one. Be aware of the disturbance which can be caused by loud church bells at night! Always give a time of arrival when you make the booking. If you think you might be later than the time indicated, make sure you telephone to warn the hotel. Otherwise, your room might be given to someone else. Written confirmation of the booking can also be useful. Do this by post or fax. As elsewhere in France, you can also stay in *gîtes* (rural cottages) or *chambres d'hôte* (bed and breakfast rooms). You will find a list of these addresses at the town hall or *office du tourisme*.

RESTAURANTS

It is a good idea to book in advance, both to be certain that you have a table, and to be sure that the restaurant is open on that particular day. It is always best to choose the *plat du jour* (menu of the day), not only because it is always cheaper than *à la carte* but also because the dishes on the menu are often made from ingredients fresh from the market. In simple restaurants, it makes sense to choose regional dishes because the cook will probably find these easier than complicated recipes from elsewhere.

Choose regional wines and, when possible, ones from the village itself; these will have been more critically and selected than wines from other regions. Tap water is always available free but you can also order still or sparkling bottled water.

Above *Château de Crémat in the minute and exclusive appellation of Bellet; these wines are mainly sold to wealthy Côte d'Azur residents.*

WINEGROWERS

Most Provençal wine producers are organised for selling to private individuals, so passing trade is normally welcome. You will be even more welcome if you show a real interest in wine; showing them a copy of this guide could help. It means that you may be offered better and more expensive *cuvées* to taste, which would not be offered to just any passer-by. When tasting wine it is customary to spit out the wine, either into a special bowl or bucket, or outside on the ground.

Out of courtesy you should ask the owner whether it is all right to do this. You should also ask what you should do with the left-over wine in the glass because sometimes the producer pours the remains into a special container. Never tip wine producers, but do buy at least one bottle as a token of gratitude for their hospitality – or several if they have been generous with the tastings. On the whole, French is the only language spoken by winegrowers, although nowadays the younger wine producers sometimes speak English as well.

MAPS

All accompanying maps in this book are designed to assist the wine traveller in following the routes recommended in the text. Relevant villages and wine towns are clearly marked to make your journey simpler and more enjoyable.

PLACES OF INTEREST

Provence is steeped in history and cultural interest. Details of the more interesting places to visit in the surrounding local areas are included, as well as special attractions and events that may be of interest.

Les Baux-de-Provence

What were once the seven westernmost *communes* of the AOC Coteaux d'Aix-en-Provence are now allowed to distinguish themselves separately; their title is Les Baux-de-Provence. Both Coteaux d'Aix and Les Baux have only been promoted to illustrious AOC status in the past 15 years, and this is undoubtedly a reflection of a determined effort on the part of wine producers to improve wine quality in this part of Provence. Les Baux-de-Provence has been a full *appellation contrôlée* since 1995. Prior to that, it was incorporated as a section of Coteaux d'Aix-en-Provence and had to use both names on the label. Before 1985, it was a VDQS (*vin delimité de qualité supérieure*) under the name Coteaux-des-Baux-de-Provence.

The smallest domaine in Les Baux-de-Provence has just under five hectares of vineyards, while the largest (Mas de la Dame) has almost 60; these vineyards are overshadowed by Les Alpilles, a grey and rugged mountain range which is surrounded by flatter plateaux. The soil here is chalky, with a top layer of clay and stones. In the area as a whole, red grape varieties predominate, including Grenache, Syrah, Mourvèdre, Cinsaut and Cabernet Sauvignon (officially up to a maximum of 20 per cent).

As a result, this is predominantly a red wine region, unlike Côtes de Provence, where the bulk of the production is rosé. Both reds and rosé may be sold as Les Baux-de-Provence but the small number of white wines produced here are not entitled to the appellation, and are sold as Coteaux d'Aix-en-Provence. The best Baux red wines are meaty and rich tasting with an attractive fruity aroma of red and black berries, plus hints of woodsmoke and spice. Wine writers are generally enthusiastic about their quality and reliability; some consider these red wines the best in Provence, representing good value for money,

Left *The historic citadel town of Les Baux-de-Provence seems almost to grow out of the rocky landscape.*

Above *The rugged lower slopes of Les Alpilles are host to flocks of sheep; lamb is a local delicacy.*

when compared with higher priced offerings from older appellations such as Bandol. They are also notable for including noble grape varieties such as Cabernet Sauvignon and Syrah in the blend instead of traditional, duller Mourvèdre or Cinsaut. This will be an area to watch for in the future.

In general, grapes in the Les Baux region are very much overshadowed by olives, which are pressed at cooperatives and by private producers to make olive oil. This is the heartland of the olive in France, and there is even a museum dedicated to them, at Les Baux-de-Provence. Some 7,000 hectares are planted with olive trees, yielding about 500 tonnes of oil annually; all pressed by local cooperatives. A visit to one of these can make a change from wine-tasting! Another speciality of the region is lamb from Les Alpilles, delicious with a red Les Baux-de-Provence wine.

The route described in this chapter starts in Salon-de-Provence, which is actually located in the *appellation contrôlée* Coteaux d'Aix-en-Provence, and continues through the *communes* of Eygalières, St-Rémy-de-Provence, Les Baux-de-Provence itself, Maussane-les-Alpilles and Mouriès. The other three *communes* of the AOC Les Baux-de-Provence are Fontvieille and St-Etienne-du-Grès to the west of the

Above *These presses at Mouriès are not for grapes but olives; olive oil cooperatives play an important part in the local economy.*

Bégude
Céreste

Manosque
la Bastide-
des-Jourdans
Sisteron
St-Martin-
de-la-Brasque
Beaumont-
de-Pertuis
la Tour-
d'Aigues
Mirabeau
Pertuis
St-Paul-
les-Durance
Peyrolles-
en-Provence
Meyrargues
VAR
Rians
CHÂTEAU
VIGNELAURE
Vauvenargues
Brignoles

Département boundary

•   Wine commune

■ CHÂTEAU   Major producer

    Côtes du Lubéron

    Coteaux d'Aix-en-Provence

    Les Baux-de-Provence

    Palette

    Wine route

Above *The picturesque Château de Calissanne is located in the warm southern zone of Les Baux-de-Provence; red wines are made here with Cabernet Sauvignon and Syrah, and aged in wood.*

Below *Oak trees and vines at the organic Mas de Gourgonnier estate.*

LES BAUX-DE-PROVENCE

RECOMMENDED PRODUCERS

EYGUIERES

Domaine des Glauges
Small *domaine* with good wines,
such as the red Rêve de Pierres,
rosé Instant Passion and white
Emotion Coteaux d'Aix-en-Provence.

EYGALIERES

Domaine d'Eole
Commendable red and rosé wines.
Domaine de la Vallongue
Produces mainly red Les Baux, as
well as a little rosé. The grapes
are grown organically.

ST-REMY-DE-PROVENCE

Domaine des Terres Blanches
Organically aware *domaine* with
an excellent reputation. Produces
a range of red wines, including
the Cuvée Aurélia with Cabernet
Sauvignon and Syrah; also makes
white and rosé wines.

ST-ETIENNE-DU-GRES

Domaine de Trévallon
Top of the range Les Baux-de-
Provence winegrower, producing
intense red wines, full of herbal
nuances, made from Cabernet
Sauvignon and Syrah. Winemaker
Eloi Durbach is justly admired for his
distinctive wines but the red may only
be called Vin de Pays des Bouches du
Rhône because of its high proportion
of Cabernet. He also makes a small
amount of white from Marsanne.

LES BAUX-DE-PROVENCE

Mas de la Dame
The largest wine estate of this region.
Makes red, rosé and white of various
qualities. Do taste the red wine
Cuvée de la Stèle.
Mas Ste-Berthe
Acknowledged as one of the
important growers for Les Baux-de-
Provence, this estate cultivates five
red and three white grape varieties.
The red Cuvée Louis David is made
from Cabernet Sauvignon, Syrah and
Grenache, aged in new casks.

MOURIES

Mas de Gourgonnier
One of the larger *domaines*. The
best red is the Réserve du Mas, a
rich, meaty wine; the white is also
interesting.and well-balanced.

LANCON-PROVENCE

Château de Calissanne
This substantial property produces
500,000 bottles annually. The red
Cuvée Prestige is an excellent wine,
and the rosé and white are also good.

town of Les Baux-de-Provence. Nestling amid olive groves, the town of Salon-de-Provence is an excellent starting point to embark on a tour around the nearby vineyards of Les Baux-de-Provence. Salon has a picturesque old town centre which was once surrounded by fortified walls; all that remains now are two ancient gates on the north side of the town, the Porte Bourg-Neuf (13th century) and the Porte de l'Horloge (17th century).

The old centre is partly surrounded by three shaded *cours* (promenades), and has an attractive town hall built in the style of an Italian *palazzo*. Opposite stands a fountain and a statue of Adam de Craponne, an engineer born in Salon who organised construction of the irrigation canal, bringing water to this arid part of Provence.

The Château de l'Empéri, former residence of the archbishops of Arles, is built on a rock towering above the historic town centre. Steps lead up to the castle, parts of which date back to the 13th century; and which is now a national military museum. The collegiate church of St-Laurent is the most beautiful in Salon and an excellent example of Provençal Gothic; Louis XIV described it as 'the most beautiful church in my kingdom'.

Left *Vines almost at the limit of the tree line in the Alpilles mountain range; Mas de la Dame, Les Baux.*

HOTELS

Auberge Provençale
Eygalières
Tel: 4 90 95 91 00
Charming little hotel in the centre of the town with a terrace at the back. Lunch and dinner are served on the terrace when weather permits. Comfortable rooms.

La Benvengudo
Les Baux-de-Provence
Tel: 4 90 54 32 54
Large building, peaceful location, in a park at the foot of the old village. Twenty rooms, elegantly furnished. Swimming pool and good restaurant.

Crin Blanc
Eygalières
Tel: 4 90 95 93 17
Pretty hotel with 10 rooms, modern furnishings. The restaurant offers an excellent Provençal menu. Tennis court and swimming pool.

Mas du Soleil
38 Chemin St-Cône
Salon-de-Provence
Tel: 4 90 56 06 53
Centrally situated yet peaceful hotel with garden and swimming pool. Ten pretty rooms full of character. The hotel's restaurant, François Robin, is the best locally and also has delicious regional wines.

L'Oustaloun
Maussane-les-Alpilles
Tel: 4 90 54 32 19
In the church square, this hotel (with 10 rooms) overlooks a large fountain. Regional dishes at reasonable prices, served in the vaulted dining room.

RESTAURANTS

Le Bistrot des Alpilles
15 Boulevard Mirambeau
St-Rémy-de-Provence
Tel: 4 90 92 09 17
Fun place to have lunch, popular locally. Delicious leg of lamb and grilled dishes. In sunny weather, meals are served on the terrace.

Salon-de-Provence was the home town of the noted healer and astrologer Nostradamus, who lived at the court of Catherine de Médici in the 16th century. His predictions are still published and discussed to this day.

From Salon-de-Provence take the D17 to Eyguières, a wine-producing village with Roman origins. There is an interesting wall painting next to the town hall, and by the main car park are steps leading through a gate to a ruined castle. From Eyguières you can walk to the highest point of Les Alpilles (493 metres); at the top stands the Tour des Opies giving a fabulous panoramic view.

Continue along the D17 to the little village of Aureille and from there take the D25 along a scenic route to Eygalières, an attractive village set below a crumbling château. Also worth visiting is the Romanesque chapel of St-Sixte (out of the village toward Orgon). Continue on to St-Rémy-de-Provence by taking the N99 past four winegrowing domaines, including Terres Blanches.

St-Rémy itself is a charming place with picturesque streets and a typically Provençal ambience. Exhibitions of contemporary art are sometimes organised at the 18th-century Hôtel Estrine, which also houses a collection of

L'Oustau de Baumanière
Les Baux-de-Provence
Tel: 4 90 54 33 07
One of France's best restaurants
where traditional, Provençal dishes
are prepared with great refinement.
Impressive wine list. Also has some
25 luxuriously furnished rooms.
Park, swimming pool, tennis courts.

Relais du Coche
Eyguières
Tel: 4 90 59 86 70
Pleasant restaurant with several
good fish specialities.

La Salle à Manger
6 Rue du Maréchal-Joffre
Salon-de-Provence
Tel: 4 90 56 28 01
Elegant restaurant with Italianate
decor, offering excellent cuisine
(leave room for pudding). Two-
course lunches are also available.

PLACES OF INTEREST

● The *Musée Vieil Eygalières* is
housed in the 17th-century Chapelle
des Pénitents.
● An olive museum is situated in
the Romanesque chapel of St Blaise
at Les Baux-de-Provence.
● There are several golf courses
in the area including one at Salon-
de-Provence (18 holes), Les Baux-
de-Provence (9 holes) and Mouriès
(in the nearby hamlet of Servanne,
18 holes).

LOCAL ATTRACTIONS

● Tuesday is market day in Eyguières
and Lançon-de-Provence.
● A Friday morning market is held
in Eygalières and Mouriès.
● Mouriès holds an Olive Fair during
the third weekend in September.
● Markets are held on Tuesday,
Friday and Saturday mornings in
Salon-de-Provence.
● Wednesday and Saturday
morning markets are held in
St-Rémy-de-Provence.
● Maussane-les-Alpilles holds a
market on Thursdays. It also stages
a wine festival during the first
weekend of October, in the place
de l'Eglise.

Van Gogh memorabilia. Regional history and traditions
come to life at the *Musée des Alpilles*, while those interested
in archeology will be fascinated by the *Musée Archéologique*.
Many of its treasures were discovered in Glanum, an ancient
Roman town about one kilometre south of St-Rémy,
which is particularly well preserved.

Drive on beyond these Roman remains on the D5 and
follow signs for Les Baux-de-Provence. The roads outside
the village are always lined with parked cars, even out of
season, but this is mainly due to the steep charges levied in
the official car parks. Around one million tourists go to
Les Baux every year to see the village and visit the ruins
of an impressive citadel nearby; both the village and the
citadel are built on a rocky outcrop which dominates the
surrounding countryside. This was once a source of soft
stone much favoured by sculptors. It is also where bauxite
(aluminium ore) was discovered, and mines were established
here as long ago as 1822.

Right *Les Baux-de-Provence is
crowned by an 11th-century citadel
which can only be reached on foot.*

In the narrow streets of Les Baux you will find at least six museums, covering subjects which include *santons* (traditional Provençal painted clay figurines); the circus; medieval books; contemporary Provençal art and local history. If all this culture proves tiring, take refuge in one of the local restaurants; this town is renowned for its food.

In the past, Les Baux had 6,000 inhabitants and the castle was inhabited by the local *seigneurs*. They were extremely powerful with a fiefdom extending over more than 70 villages in southern France; their history is marked by wars, intrigues and betrayals, but they also organised elegant feasts and banquets and often offered their hospitality to wandering troubadours. The end of the dynasty signified the end of the castle which was demolished in 1632 on the orders of Louis XIII. Among its ruins several towers still survive, as well as a dungeon, a hospital and two chapels.

Below the village are several vineyards, including Mas Ste-Berthe and Mas de la Dame. Olives vie with grapes for land here; there is an olive oil cooperative at Maussane-Les-Alpilles, and Mouriès, the next village to the east, is the largest olive growing commune in France.

Before returning to Salon-de-Provence, stop briefly at Lançon-Provence. Although surrounded by modern housing developments, this hilltop town is dominated by a 14th-century castle with ruined fortifications.

Above *A relaxing setting for a well-earned break in the historic town of St-Rémy-de-Provence.*

43

Coteaux d'Aix-en-Provence

The wine region of Coteaux d'Aix-en-Provence stretches across some 3,700 hectares and includes at least 40 *communes*. These are all in the *département* of the Bouches-du-Rhône, with the exception of Artigues and Rians in the Var. It was in Rians that Georges Brunet planted this region's first Cabernet Sauvignon vinestocks at his domaine, Château Vignelaure. Brunet came from Bordeaux where he had managed Château La Lagune; he cultivated his vines organically, without weedkillers or insecticides. The experiment was a resounding success and Cabernet Sauvignon was officially accepted for the *appellation contrôlée* Coteaux d'Aix-en-Provence.

Below *Visit the château of La Barben for its gardens and zoo as well as its lushly furnished interiors.*

44

This appellation was actually awarded after that of Côtes de Provence. To the great disappointment of the winegrowers around Aix-en-Provence, their region was not promoted when Côtes de Provence was given its *appellation contrôlée* in 1977. They had to wait until 1985 to be upgraded; the reason given by Paris for this delay was the 'heterogeneity' of the vineyards, producing rather a mixed bag of wines.

Today Coteaux d'Aix-en-Provence is a significant wine region which makes attractive wines. About half of the wines are rosé and over 40 per cent red. Many red wines owe a large part of their character and distinction to the Cabernet Sauvignon grape, and are vinified in a deliberately light style for early drinking. The characteristic flavour of these wines includes hints of balsam and game. The white wines, at present only five per cent of the production, are becoming increasingly interesting; many include Sémillon or Sauvignon Blanc, in addition to the more traditional 'workhorse' grape of the region, Ugni Blanc.

RECOMMENDED PRODUCERS

AURONS
Château Petit Sonnallier
An 18th-century château with 12th-century origins, in an attractive forest setting,, producing well-made rosé.

VERNEGUES
Château Bas
Also the site of an ancient temple; the best wine is the red Cuvée du Temple, made with Cabernet Sauvignon and Syrah, admired for its smooth style and keeping qualities.

LAMBESC
Château de Calavon
This former château of the Princes of Orange has vineyards with chalky soil, yielding good-quality red wines, notably the Cuvée Spéciale.
Domaine des Béates
Formerly a convent, this is now an organic *domaine* producing various qualities of wine. The white Clos St-Eldrad is a pleasant surprise. The rosé Réserve du Grand Ecuyer is a feast for the senses.

ST-CANNAT
Château de Beaupré
A bastide surrounded by an enormous park, dating from 1739; the vineyard was established in 1890. The white wines are aged in new oak casks to give a rich style like that of Bordeaux. One of the top estates in the Coteaux d'Aix-en-Provence.
Commanderie de la Bargemonne
Very reliable. Cuvée Tournebride is its best red wine.

ROGNES
Château de Beaulieu
As the name suggests, the estate is beautifully situated in woodland, producing good rosé and white wines, and Cabernet Sauvignon reds.
Château Barbebelle
Produces white Cuvée Jas d'Amour, made with Sauvignon Blanc, red Cuvée Réserve, and pleasant rosé.

LE PUY-STE-REPARADE
Château la Coste
A large estate with a good range of wines. One of the best is the white Cuvée Lisa. The Blanc de blancs is also of good quaity.
Château de Fonscolombe
Pure, elegant Coteaux d'Aix-en-Provence (Cuvée Spéciale is the best red) and other wines, including agreeable *vins de pays*. Ask in the shop to view the château and park.
Domaine Les Bastides
The red Cuvée Spéciale is recommended.

Both white and rosé wines are light and delicate in this area; growers ascribe their quality to the location of the vineyards which are sheltered from the damaging *mistral* winds. The charmingly-named *rosé d'une nuit* is literally fermented with red grapeskins for one night only, resulting in a subtle colour and corresponding lightness in the wine.

The route described here will take you through some of the most beautiful parts of this wine region, and direct you to the cellars of some excellent producers. The town of Aix-en-Provence is dealt with separately (*see* page 50).

Above *The striking 14th-century octagonal bell tower of Lambesc's church dominates the skyline.*
Right *The courtyard of Château Vignelaure, once the home of vine pioneer Georges Brunet.*

Far right *The Château du Seuil in Puyricard has 13th-century origins; today the estate produces fine red, rosé and white wines.*

BETWEEN SALON AND AIX-EN-PROVENCE

Take the D16 from Salon-de-Provence in a northwesterly direction to Aurons. After driving along a twisting road through wooded hills and crossing a barren plateau you finally reach this small, quiet village, with its tiny Romanesque church. The history of the village is recorded on a panel nearby. In the neighbouring old village of Vieux-Vernègues you can see the ruins of the houses and Romanesque church destroyed by an earthquake; in clear weather the view from here is spectacular.

Now follow the D22, first south, then east towards Cazan, and you will come to Château Bas. This estate attracts countless visitors, not just because of its good wines and its attractive castle, but also to see the ruins of a Roman temple, on a low hill behind the château.

In Cazan, take the N7 to Lambesc, a large village with over 6,000 inhabitants. Lambesc played an important part in the history of Provence; it was here, for instance, that the Provençal parliament met. The town still boasts some magnificent houses from that period (16th to 18th century) and a fine church with an octagonal bell tower. A short distance away is another bell tower of polished white stone which was once a gate in the town walls; there are turtles swimming in the small fountain opposite. You can see more of Lambesc's rich history in the *Musée du Vieux-Lambesc*.

The winegrowing village of St-Cannat suffers from the traffic on the N7. The route continues towards Rognes, along the D18 which traverses a small mountain ridge. Entering the village it is evident that Rognes has another speciality besides wine: ochre-coloured stone. The parish church looks rather austere from the outside but the interior is truly sumptuous with some magnificent altarpieces and columns decorated with vine shoots. A little distance away from the present-day village centre are the chapel and hermitage of St-Marcellin. They date respectively from the 12th and 14th century and have been carefully restored; a harvest blessing and supper takes place here on the second Sunday of September.

PUYRICARD

Château du Seuil
The oldest part of the castle dates from the 13th century. The vines are cultivated at quite a high altitude. Wines produced include an attractive Blanc Prestige and a fragrant rosé, as well as various red wines.

Domaine de St-Julien les Vignes
Good red wines and characterful white wines are made at this *domaine*, which occupies an 18th-century bastide.

MEYRARGUES

Château de Vauclaire
The rosé here is made from 100% Grenache grapes, giving it an orangey colour and a nose of dried apricots.

JOUQUES

Château Revelette
Producers of expensive wines, aged in wood, including Le Grand Blanc and Le Grand Rouge.

Domaine de la Grande Séouve
Produces, among others, an excellent red wine aged in wood.

RIANS

Château Pigoudet
The red Cuvée de la Chapelle is an extremely pleasant wine, made using both Cabernet Sauvignon and Syrah grapes, and there is also a good rosé. The château here was built on the foundations of an old Roman villa. Note the ancient cedars of Lebanon in the surrounding woods.

Château Vignelaure
The red wine produced at this estate, already much admired, has improved considerably since the beginning of the 1990s, under the guidance of Hugh Ryman, a well-known English 'flying winemaker' who had already transformed several wines of the French southwest. The red wine of Château Vignelaure is made from four grape varieties. La Source de Vignelaure is the producer's second wine, both red and rosé, fruity and full in style. Among others, the name Domaine de Vignelaure is used for the Vin de Pays du Var, which is made with Cabernet Sauvignon only and has a bouquet of blackberries. In the cellars, the walls are hung with art works among the wine barrels.

HOTELS

Le Bois St-Hubert
Rians
Tel: 4 94 80 31 00
Small tastefully furnished hotel, in
extensive grounds, on the D3. Quiet
location. Swimming pool and terrace.
The chic restaurant offers delicious,
sophisticated dishes.

Le Mas des Ecureuils
Quartier Valcros
Les Milles
Aix-en-Provence
Tel: 4 42 24 40 48
The small suburb of Les Milles is
south-west of Aix. It can be reached
by *autoroute*, direction Marseille. Make
sure you follow the road signs. The
hotel is built on a wooded hill with
25 rooms in a series of small, simple
bungalows. The hotel's restaurant,
La Carraire, serves fairly simple food.

RESTAURANTS

Les Olivarelles
Rognes
Tel: 4 42 50 24 27
Country inn serving traditional
cuisine, such as rabbit dishes.

Le Réal
Jouques
Tel: 4 42 67 60 85
Pleasant village restaurant with a
country atmosphere, specialising in
traditional, regional dishes and game.

Les Souvenirs d'Avenir
Rians
Tel: 4 94 80 50 15
Overlooking a small square with a
fountain, in the centre of Rians, not
far from the church. In fine weather
you can eat outside. Country cooking,
reasonably priced.

LOCAL ATTRACTIONS

● La Barben: on the D572 between
S:alon and St-Cannat, a château with
exquisite furniture and tapestries. and
a beautiful garden designed by
Lenôtre. There is also a zoo which
includes a rare white rhinoceros.
● Aix-en-Provence: Music festivals are
held here during July and August.

LOCAL MARKETS

● Lambesc holds a market on Friday.
● Wednesday is market day in
Rognes and Meyargues
● Le Puy-Ste-Réparade and Jouques
hold their markets on Sunday.

In certain years, the vignerons of Rognes stage a special
banquet in the middle of July, dedicated to the Coteaux
d'Aix-en-Provence *appellation contrôlée*.

From Rognes make a small detour to the Château de
Beaulieu, a domaine with an attractive château surrounded
by woods and vineyards producing excellent wines. On the
way back you could also stop at the much-advertised
Château Barbebelle which is one of the oldest winegrowing
estates in the Aix area.

Journey on along the D15 to Le Puy-St-Réparade, a
rather dull village redeemed by its excellent wine-
producing estates. The best-known is the Château de
Fonscolombe, a few kilometres east of the village on the
D13. Generally visitors are only allowed to visit the cellar
and the shop, but it is worthwhile asking whether you can
visit the castle (renovated in the 19th century) surrounded
by lush parkland.

From Le Puy-Ste-Réparade, take the D14 to the village
of Puyricard, which has a picturesque Romanesque church
with an attractive open bell tower. There are several wine
estates in easy reach of this village, among them Château du
Seuil, but most visitors come for tastings at the nearby
chocolate factory, said to make the best chocolates in
France. From Puyricard, the D15 will lead you directly to
Aix-en-Provence, but if you would like to spend a little

Top left *The vine is celebrated at the heart of life here in Rognes; several festivals are devoted to wine.*

Left *The stylish Château de Fonscolombe was built in the last century and has a fairytale quality; the estate also produces some top-quality Coteaux d'Aix red wine.*

more time in the vineyards, go back to Le Puy-Ste-Réparade and take the N96 to Meyrargues, staying on this route through the town of Peyrolles, which is notable for its 17th-century castle, nowadays used as the *mairie* (town hall). Turn off towards Jouques onto the D561, or a little further on take the D61, a narrower but more scenic road with several picturesque gardens en route. The noted wine domaines of Château Vignelaure and Château Pigoudet are in this area. Retrace your steps to Peyrolles, and take the main N96 road for a rapid ride to Aix-en-Provence.

HOTELS

Hôtel des Quatre Dauphins
54 Rue Roux-Alphéran
Tel: 4 42 38 16 39
A dozen pretty rooms in a building
only 150 metres from the Cours
Mirabeau. No restaurant.

Mercure Paul Cézanne
40 Avenue Victor Hugo
Tel: 4 42 23 29 23
Centrally located and well furnished,
this hotel serves breakfast only; for
other meals use nearby restaurants.

AIX-EN-PROVENCE

In 122BC the Roman Consul Sextius founded a settlement near some natural springs about 30 kilometres north of Marseilles and named it Aquae Sextius, or Aix-en-Provence as it is now known. Today, the city is surrounded by autoroutes and dull, sprawling suburbs, yet the old centre has an unmistakable elegance, with impressive town houses, picturesque streets and attractive squares. Art plays an important part in the life of the city with a variety of annual art festivals. Paul Cézanne was born here in 1839 and his presence is still felt in Aix: a special walk devoted to the painter has been devised for visitors. It starts at the *office du tourisme* (Place Général de Gaulle) and takes in his paintings

at the Musée Granet, as well as the house where he died in 1906. A little further from the centre, in the northern part of the city, is Cézanne's *atélier*, or work studio, appropriately located in the avenue Paul-Cézanne.

The Cours Mirabeau is a striking feature of the city centre. It is an extended square, spacious and shady, each side lined with the tall plane trees that are typical of Provence. On its north side is a row of shops, restaurants and cafés, among them the famous Les Deux Garçons. The Cours Mirabeau is the meeting-place of Aix-en-Provence, and has been since 1792. Paul Cézanne often came here, as did Jean Cocteau and Emile Zola. In its centre is a moss-covered fountain which dates back to Roman times,

RESTAURANTS

Les Deux Garçons
53 Cours Mirabeau
Tel: 4 42 23 30 71
Famous for its literary clientele and good brasserie food. Not cheap.

Les Bacchanales
10 Rue Couronne
Tel: 4 42 27 21 06
Inventive cuisine, both rich and sophisticated. An excellent address for lunch and dinner in the old town.

Below Each Sunday the central square in Aix is transformed into a colourful and fragrant flower market.

Le Mazerin
13 Cours Mirabeau
Tel: 4 42 27 62 86
Good for *coquillages* (shellfish).

Brasserie Léopold
2 Avenue Victor Hugo
Tel: 4 42 26 01 24
Wide choice of dishes at reasonable prices, including *choucroute* and the best steak tartare in Aix. Good wine of the month. Always full.

Chez Maxime
12 Place Ramus
Tel: 4 42 26 28 51
Centrally located restaurant with more than 500 wines in its cellar. Specialises in meat dishes and also has an attractive lunch menu.

Le Clos de la Violette
10 Avenue Violette
Tel: 4 42 23 30 71
A tastefully furnished interior and mouth-watering dishes make it a real treat to come and eat here. Advance booking is advised.

Below Would-be paddlers beware: this fountain is fed by hot water.
Top right The charm of the old stone building complements the familiar local landscapes by Paul Cézanne at this Aix poster shop.
Right 'Les Deux Garçons' café, Aix's most famous rendezvous.

spouting hot spring water (34°C). The south side of the Cours Mirabeau is much quieter, with elegant, patrician houses, while to the west, the entrance to the square is marked by an impressive round fountain dating from 1860. To the east stands a statue of *le bon roi René,* who lived in the 15th century; the last Count of Provence and also the King of Sicily, he is said to have spoken six languages and was also versed in geology, mathematics and the law, as well as being a painter, poet, musician and viticulturalist. King René is reputed to have introduced the Muscat grape to Provence and this statue depicts him holding a bunch of grapes. Behind the Cours Mirabeau (north side) is a maze of narrow streets crammed with shops, churches, squares and museums.

The *Musée du Vieil Aix* illustrates the history of the city and also contains a collection of marionettes and dolls. Opposite the cathedral of St-Sauveur (which has a curious blend of styles but is worth visiting to see its art treasures) is the *Musée des Tapisseries*, an impressive tapestry collection housed in the former Archbishop's Palace. Next to the cathedral is a Romanesque cloister and a baptismal chapel. In the *hôtel de ville* is the Méjanes Library which is open to the public. It has over 300,000 books and manuscripts, among them a richly illustrated work dedicated to King René.

There is an interesting flea-market in the place de Verdun on Tuesday, Thursday and Saturday mornings; on Sundays it becomes the *marché aux fleurs* (flower market).

Palette and the Western Côtes de Provence

Slightly east of Aix-en-Provence lies the smallest wine region in Provence: Palette. Blessed with an outcrop of limestone, it has always produced fine wine and was one of the first Provençal districts to gain *appellation contrôlée* status. The most famous, indeed virtually the only, estate here is Château Simone where red wines are made in a traditional style with excellent potential for bottle ageing; they are usually described as hard or tough since they need some years in bottle to give of their best. When mature they have a resiny flavour, and some of the austere character of a red Bordeaux. White and rosé wines from this appellation also attract favourable reviews; like the reds they are made with traditional local grape varieties.

The Palette area is also a gateway to some spectacular mountainous landscape along the ridge of the Montagne Ste-Victoire to the peak of the Massif de la Ste-Baume. Travelling east, this tour includes the south-eastern corner of the Côteaux d'Aix-en-Provence around the small wine town of Trets, then traverses the plateau towards St-Maximin-la-Ste-Baume, marking the beginnings of the Coteaux Varois appellation.

Palette is only a short distance from Aix-en-Provence; take the N7 in the direction of Fréjus and turn off on the D58 towards Meyreuil. Soon you will see a road sign indicating Château Simone, a well-maintained castle built some 400 years ago, and renovated in the last century. Today it still commands a fine view of the vineyards but the modern world has encroached in the form of the A8 autoroute nearby. The casual visitor may call at Château Simone, and it is a good place to buy a souvenir bottle, if you can make your way past the guard dogs at the gate.

Left The manicured exterior of Château Simone, AOC Palette, restored in the 19th century.

Above The towering silhouette of the Croix de Lorraine, set high on the Montagne Ste-Victoire.

PALETTE

RECOMMENDED PRODUCERS

MEYREUIL

Château Simone
This château, with cellars dating back
to the 16th century, belongs to the
Roudier family which succeeded in
creating the Palette *appellation
contrôlée* in 1948. It produces
traditional red wines which need
ageing in bottle, and meaty whites
which are full of character. The rosé
is less interesting. The domaine will
sell to passers-by but do not be
deterred by warning notices and
barking dogs. The vineyard occupies
about 17ha.

LE THOLONET

Château Crémade
Attractively sited 6ha of vineyards
produce, good, clean wines: red, rosé
and white. The best are sold under
the label Cuvée Antoinette and are
matured in cask.

RESTAURANT

La Petite Auberge du Tholonet
Le Tholonet
Tel: 4 42 66 84 24
Idyllically situated on a hillside
overlooking the wine domaine
Château Crémade. Flowery interior
and a terrace; serves good local
dishes such as *rougets de beurre
au basilic*. This is the best place to
drink Palette.

COTES DE PROVENCE

RECOMMENDED PRODUCERS

PUYLOUBIER

Château Baron Georges
Close to the Montagne Ste-Victoire;
it makes Coteaux Varois as well.
Try the full-flavoured red and rosé
Côtes de Provence.
Coopérative
Producing good examples of the local
Côtes de Provence style.
Domaine Richeaume
Tastefully laid-out *domaine* producing
superior wines organically, among
them rosé, red Cabernet Sauvignon
and red Syrah.
Domaine de St-Ser
Situated at the foot of the Montagne
Ste-Victoire, this *domaine* makes
stylish red Côtes de Provence and
a delicious rosé.

POURRIERES

Domaine Silvy
Source of an interesting red wine
with a spicy nose and potential for
keeping over several years.

Meyreuil itself is too close to a large, smoking factory to
have much rustic charm, but Le Tholonet, on the other
side of the N7 and the *autoroute*, is far more attractive. This
small village, built on a hill, has a charming, shady park and
a 17th-century castle. Look out for Château Crémade, a
well-regarded estate producing interesting wines, just before
you reach the village.

Cézanne used to paint around Le Tholonet, thus the
main street is inevitably called Avenue Cézanne, and the
local café–restaurant is the Relais Cézanne. You are now in
the foothills of the Montagne Ste-Victoire, immortalised in
so many of his paintings, and the next stage of this route
follows the D17 along the Route Cézanne.

FROM STE-VICTOIRE TO STE-BAUME

From Le Tholonet, the road winds along the southern flank
of the Montagne Ste-Victoire, with a rough, grey-white
mass of rock to the left and rolling foothills to the right.
The Montagne Ste-Victoire is not a single peak but a range
of mountains extending for about 12 kilometres to the east.
The first village *en route* is Beaureceuil, which is
recommended mainly for its pleasant hotels and restaurants,
and further along the D17 is the Parc de Roques-Hautes, a

Left *A glorious setting for the vines of Château Crémade; the limestone behind is a reminder that this is the source of quality for AOC Palette.* Below left *A sunlit corner for the parched traveller who comes to taste wines at Château Crémade, not far from the abbey of Le Tholonet.*

TRETS

Château Coussin
A beautifully maintained château, making excellent red wines with ageing potential and good rosés.

Château Ferry-Lacombe
Try the red, white and rosé Cuvée Lou Pascal. The second label is marketed under the name Les Hauts de Lacombe.

Château Grand'Boise
The special *cuvées* produced by this hillside wine estate, such as the red and white wines labelled Cuvée Mazanine, are significantly better than their ordinary wines.

Mas de Cadenet
The rosé Mas Negrel Cadenet is vinified in wood vats, which gives it quite a personality of its own. Try its white wine, which is a classic example of the genre; scented and mouth-filling.

POURCIEUX

Château de Pourcieux
Fascinating château and formal gardens. Its white wine is said to taste of bananas; try it for yourself.

ST-MAXIMIN-LA-STE-BAUME

Domaine du Deffends
Do taste the exquisite Clos de la Truffière, a red wine based on Cabernet Sauvignon and Syrah.

Domaine de St-Jean-le-Vieux
Recommended for its red Cuvée du Grand Clos. The white Vin de Pays du Var is also worth discovering.

NANS-LES-PINS

Domaine de Triennes
Two talented winegrowers from Burgundy produce a series of excellent wines here (all Vin de Pays du Var). Les Auréliens is a lively combination of Cabernet Sauvignon and Syrah. They also produce a pure Syrah, and since 1991 Chardonnay Clos Barry; also an excellent Viognier.

starting-point for many mountain walks. For the finest views, stop at the Croix de Provence, set on a summit about 1,000 metres above the valley floor. The iron cross itself is almost 20 metres tall and commemorates the gratitude of the Provençal people for being spared foreign occupation during the Franco-Prussian War in the 19th century. From this viewpoint, look for the Montagne du Lubéron and Mont Ventoux to the northwest, and the Massif de la Ste-Baume to the southeast.

Above The rugged and austere peaks of the Massif de la Ste-Baume, said to be the last refuge of St Mary Magdalene, who lived as a hermit.

HOTELS

Domaine de Châteauneuf
Nans-les-Pins
Tel: 4 94 78 90 06
Magnificent Relais et Châteaux hotel next to the golf course. Spacious, stylish rooms and suites. Tennis courts, swimming pool. Excellent restaurant where Provençal dishes have been re-interpreted to reflect today's taste. Meals are served inside, or outside on the shady terrace.

Mas de la Bertrande
Beaureceuil
Tel: 4 42 55 75 75
Nearly every room (10 in all) has a small terrace with a view of the Montagne Ste-Victoire. The rooms are quite spacious and comfortable. Friendly restaurant and good food. Swimming pool.

Hôtel Plaisance
St-Maximin-la-Ste-Baume
Tel: 4 94 78 16 74
In the centre of town, this hotel has 13 rooms, furnished in a modern style. Ask for a room at the back. Friendly service.

Relais Ste-Victoire
Beaureceuil
Tel: 4 42 66 94 98
Small hotel with ten rooms and suites furnished in classic style. Swimming pool. Pleasant dining room serving sophisticated regional dishes.

Drive on through the hamlet of St-Antonin-sur-Bayon and on towards Puyloubier; the vines spread out below marking the beginning of the Côtes de Provence zone. Puyloubier is dominated by the ruins of a medieval castle and boasts several famous wine-producing domaines such as Domaine Richeaume. The road continues through Pourrières, nestling against the side of a hill below the ruins of the Castle of Glandève and on towards Trets.

Trets itself was a fortified town in medieval times. The centre is surrounded by the ruins of ancient town walls with square, fortified gates (14th century) and still has several medieval buildings, including a 13th-century synagogue and an austere-looking church with a partly Romanesque nave. The massive clock tower dates from the 15th century, as does the local castle. In Trets you will find road signs for Château Grand'Boise, a wine-producing domaine to the east of the town.

Continue the route on the D6 in the direction of Pourcieux. On the way you will pass Château Ferry-Lacombe, a wine-producing domaine with 15th-century origins. Pourcieux itself is rumoured to be named after the Latin for pigsties, as it was once a centre for pig breeding. Today it's worth a visit to see the Gallo-Roman burial place near the village (on the east side, La Bastide Blanche). Follow signs to St-Maximin for the Château de Pourcieux, an 18th-century walled wine estate with a fine reputation.

Between the twin mountain ranges of Ste-Victoire and Ste-Baume lies a fertile plain where all types of fruit and vegetables thrive. From Pourcieux to St-Maximin-la-Ste-Baume is a 'no man's land' for the vine as the appellation shifts from Coteaux d'Aix-en-Provence to Coteaux Varois (*see* page 77). Scenically, this is a striking journey amid the mountains; *baoumo* is an ancient Provençal word for cave, and this area has long attracted pilgrims to the cave of St Mary Magdalene. She is said to have spent the last part

Left *Weighing in the vendanges at Château Simone, Palette AOC.*

RESTAURANTS

Bar du Var
Pourrières
Tel: 4 94 78 40 08
Excellent for a simple, cheap lunch.
Serves fresh *coquillages* in season.
It is also called Chez Claude.

La Brioche Provençale
Nans-les-Pins
Tel: 4 94 78 90 38
On the road to La Ste-Baume.
Honest, affordable Provençal dishes
(but avoid the *omelette sibérienne*).
Shady outdoor terrace.

Les Cèdres
Plan d'Aups
Tel: 4 42 04 50 03
Regional cuisine with generous
portions, and reasonable prices.

Chez Nous
St-Maximin-la-Ste-Baume
Tel: 4 94 78 02 57
The best restaurant locally,
managed by the friendly Roland Paix.
Good portions and fresh ingredients
from local markets. The walls are
decorated with colourful paintings
of local villages.

Le Clos Gourmand
Trets
Tel: 4 42 61 33 72
The food here is more traditional
than the interior.

Delikatessen
Puyloubier
Tel: 4 94 78 49 01
On the south side of the village;
turn off at the cooperative. The
dishes served here are a combination
of traditional and contemporary
cuisine: the result is delicious.

Golf de la Ste-Baume
Nans-les-Pins
Tel: 4 94 78 60 12
The clubhouse welcomes non-golfers
for lunch. Delicious salads, hot dishes
and an inexpensive menu of the day.

Hôtel de France
St-Maximin-la-Ste-Baume
Tel: 4 94 78 00 14
Good, simple food, also served
outside in the garden. Also a hotel
with swimming pool. (On a busy
road, so book a room at the back).

LOCAL ATTRACTIONS

• La Provençale, in St-Maximin-la-
Ste-Baume is a large distillery which
produces *marc* and brandies.
• Trets and St-Maximin-la-Ste-Baume
hold their markets on Wednesday.

of her life as a recluse here in this isolated setting, and visitors still come by the hundreds each year to attend midnight mass on her saint's day, July 22nd.

Arriving in St-Maximin-la-Ste-Baume, it would be hard to miss its most notable edifice; the imposing Gothic basilica of Ste Marie-Madeleine. This church took approximately 240 years to build (from 1295 to 1532) and is austere in design, yet the interior is softened by the beautiful, soft light filtering through the narrow windows. Next to the church is a Dominican monastery. What was once the monastery's guest house (next to the main entrance to the basilica) has been used as the town hall ever since the French Revolution.

From St-Maximin take the N560 and D80 in the direction of the Massif de la Ste-Baume. About halfway there you pass Nans-les-Pins. This charming village has been visited by many kings (such as Francis I and Louis XIV) on pilgrimage to the cave of La Ste-Baume. Nowadays the visitors are tourists, golfers mainly, attracted by the magnificent Golf de la Ste-Baume built on the north of the town. To visit the celebrated cave, take the D80 from Nans-les-Pins to Plan d'Aups. Because of its warm, dry micro-climate this area is a haven for asthma sufferers. Wine has become a more significant product here in recent years; olives, fruit and even charcoal were once the major output of the region.

Back in Nans-les-Pins, either drive south to the coast via the D80 (a winding scenic route) and the N560 to visit the area around Cassis (*see* page 101), or opt to go east.

Côtes du Lubéron

The Côtes du Lubéron wine region begins just 20 kilometres north of Aix-en-Provence. Once a minor area, included in the Côtes du Rhône appellation, today it has been colonised by media moguls and actors with the result that the wines are far more stylish and interesting. Syrah is the favoured grape for red wines, many of which have ageing potential as well as immediate charm.

The Lubéron area is separated from Coteaux d'Aix-en-Provence by the River Durance, which also divides the *départements* of the Bouches-du-Rhône and the Vaucluse. Wine has been made here since Roman times; a sarcophagus with decorations depicting Bacchus and a bas-relief which illustrates the early wine trade in Gaul have been found in the vicinity.

The Côtes du Lubéron *appellation contrôlée* has only existed since 1988, and with its 3,500 hectares it is slightly smaller than Coteaux d'Aix-en-Provence. In contrast to its southern neighbour, production here is dominated by cooperatives which are responsible for processing over 90 per cent of the grapes; but the best wines are usually produced by private *domaines*. The itinerary described in this chapter concentrates mainly on these private winegrowing estates – with the result that it is mainly the Southern Lubéron which is covered (including Apt), because that is where the best wine-producing *domaines* are found; they make mainly red wines, ranging from fruity styles to be drunk young, to those aged in wood. The quality of the rosé and white wines is steadily improving.

The Parc Naturel Régional du Lubéron, created in 1977, runs straight through the region. It includes 51 villages or towns with 90,000 inhabitants in all, covering an area of 130,000 hectares, one-third of the entire *département* of the Vaucluse. The Montagne du Lubéron, a limestone

Left *The natural beauty of the Lubéron's wooded slopes set against neat and tidy apple trees.*

Above *Apt is a centre for production of high-quality dried fruit such as cherries, apricots and greengages.*

COTES DU LUBERON

RECOMMENDED PRODUCERS

PERTUIS
Château Grand Callamand
A large Provençal *mas* (manor house and estate) producing a rosé wine, among others.
Château Val Joanis
This large, dynamic and well-equipped family domaine produces reliable wines. The best is the red Les Griottes, a red wine aged in wood, which effectively combines the strength of Grenache with the elegance of Syrah.

PUGET-SUR-DURANCE
Château la Verrerie
Taken over in 1981 by a wealthy businessman, this operation has since been expanded and modernised, including the building of an ultra-modern cellar. Good red wine aged in large casks is produced here, as well as aromatic white wine and pleasant rosé. The second label is Bastide de Verrerie.

LOURMARIN
Château Constantin-Chevalier
Commended for fine red wines and good white, including the Cuvée des Fondateurs, fermented in oak vats.

Right *Vertiginous views down to the Durance river valley from the hillside town of Ansouis.*
Below *Even the gardens are terraced in the fortified towns of the Lubéron.*

mountain range with peaks of over 1,100 metres, rises in the middle of this natural park. Vines are cultivated on its north and south sides; alternating with the wild, natural beauty of woods, wild flowers and herbs.

DRIVING THROUGH THE LUBERON

From Aix-en-Provence, travel north on the D556 to Pertuis. This is the capital of the southern Lubéron and it was built on a hilltop; from afar its distinctive outline is marked by a bell tower and the ruins of a 12th-century castle. The church of St-Nicolas on the main square has been rebuilt several times since the 14th century; it contains many art treasures and an organ which has been declared a listed monument. There are some distinguished houses in the centre such as the 16th-century corner house named after Reine Jeanne. Walking through the town you will come across several fountains dating from the 16th to the 19th centuries; remnants of the town walls can still be seen on the south-west side of Pertuis.

From here take the D973 in the direction of Cadenet. The turning to the important winegrowing domaine of Château Val Joanis is just outside Pertuis. *En route*, there are ruins of a 16th-century castle in Villelaure; also the square-shaped complex called La Fabrique, an enormous model farm dating from 1832. Cadenet is dramatically sited beneath a rock face, on top of which are the ruins of a castle, walls and a tower, with galleries and cave dwellings hewn out of the rock on the north side. In the village square is a statue of the drummer boy of Arcole; the little bronze sculpture represents André Etienne, born in Cadenet, who as a 15-year old led his battalion into battle.

From Cadenet, wine lovers should make a small detour to Puget-sur-Durance, to visit the impressive Château la Verrerie, a wine-producing domaine which was modernised and enlarged during the 1980s. Then drive onward via the D943 to Lourmarin, one of the most beautiful villages in the Lubéron; a compact place with narrow, picturesque streets and attractive 16th- and 17th-century houses, many converted into artist's workshops and art galleries. Pretty little squares, a bell tower (built on the foundations of an older castle), an 18th-century fountain and a partly Romanesque church complete the picture. Beyond the church follow the road to the Renaissance château built by the d'Agoult family, containing fine furniture and fireplaces as well as a collection of musical instruments. Albert Camus (1913–1960), winner of the Nobel Prize for literature, is buried in the local churchyard.

Further to the north, the D943 traces the course of a gorge through the Montagne du Lubéron; turn left here on to the D36 to Bonnieux. This village is pre-Roman in origin, built on a hillside with a ruined castle and two medieval churches. Visit the *Musée de la Boulangerie* for details about the craft of breadmaking and to see an old traditional bakery. Six kilometres from the village on the

Above *The church at Lourmarin. The writer and philosopher Albert Camus is buried in the churchyard.*

BONNIEUX
Château la Canorgue
An attractive 17th-century property, near the Pont Julien. Fine red wine with plenty of fruit and spicy over-tones as well as stylish rosé and white wine. The vineyard is run organically.

APT
Château de l'Isolette
Makes a range of agreeable red, rosé and white wines; good with Provençal dishes cooked in olive oil.
Château de Mille
The floral-scented white wine is usually good, made with Clairette, Bourboulenc and Roussanne grapes in equal measure.
Domaine de Mayol
Delicious red Côtes du Lubéron.

CUCURON
Château la Sable
The attractive, light orange-tinted rosé made here goes well with local lamb dishes; also produce a classy white wine, rich and full-bodied.
Domaine de la Cavale
The white wine has an attractive colour and is very 'quaffable'.

LA TOUR D'AIGUES
Cellier de Marrenon
This is an enormous concern where the wines of more than 15 regional cooperatives are blended and bottled (under different labels) in modern cellars. Some wines are aged in wooden casks. One of the top of the range labels is Grande Toque (red, rosé and white wines).

LAURIS
Domaine de Fontenille
A family estate producing red wine.

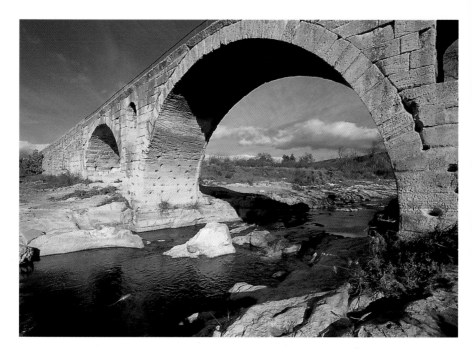

Above Almost perfectly preserved, it is hard to believe that the Pont Julien dates back to Roman times. Right The enchanting village of Lourmarin, a magnet for tourists and inhabited by numerous artists.

MIRABEAU
Clos Mirabeau
Tannic red wine and a pale yellow white wine which goes well with seafood; the latter is (confusingly) labelled as Clos Murabeau.

 HOTELS

Auberge du Lubéron
8 Place du Faubourg de Ballet
Apt
Tel: 4 90 74 12 50
Close to the old centre, with 15 reasonable rooms. Good restaurant with terrace. Regional dishes prepared with fresh ingredients. Garage.
L'Etang
Cucuron
Tel: 4 90 77 21 25
Homely village inn with eight rooms The hotel's restaurant serves delicious, traditional dishes at reasonable prices.
Hôtel de Guilles
Lourmarin
Tel: 4 90 68 30 55
On the road to Vaugines, deep in the countryside. Charming rooms. Breakfast is served in a flower-filled conservatory by the swimming pool. The restaurant features regional dishes such as shoulder of lamb.

D149 is the Pont Julien, named after Julius Caesar and one of the best preserved Roman bridges in Provence. Continue by taking the D3 from Bonnieux towards Apt. You will pass four wine-producing estates on the way: Château de l'Isolette, Château de Mille, Domaine de Mayol and Domaine des Andes. After the rural atmosphere and relative tranquillity of the places you have just visited, the hustle and bustle of Apt comes as a shock; there is a lot of traffic, partly caused by the busy nearby *route nationale*.

Only the old centre of Apt is worth visiting, to admire the cathedral of Ste-Anne with its richly ornamented décor and Romanesque tower. There are two museums in Apt: the *Musée Archéologique* (with traces of a Gallo-Roman theatre in the basement) and the *Musée de la Paléontologie* (an exhibition featuring prehistoric animals; located in the Maison du Parc).

Corkscrew collectors and enthusiasts may want to take a diversion at this point, heading east to Ménerbes which is home to a remarkable collection of *tire-bouchons*. Among the 1,000 on show are some dating back to the 17th century, and many are unique examples. Outside the Domaine de la Citadelle, which houses the collection, is a garden where examples of local vines are cultivated, and there is also a fine library of wine-related books.

Otherwise, take the D943 out of Apt towards Lourmarin. On your left, as you drive through the mountains of the Lubéron, stands the Prieuré de St-Symphorien and a restored Romanesque chapel. At Lourmarin, take the D56 to Vaugines. This ancient hamlet has a charming little church, St-Sauveur, the oldest part of which dates from the 11th century.

Le Jardin d'Ansouis
Ansouis
Tel: 4 90 09 89 27
Very good *gîte rural* in the old village (not far from the car park). Has only two rooms. Serve dinner on request; in the summer, they have a tea room.

Le Moulin de Lourmarin
Lourmarin
Tel: 4 90 68 06 69
Magnificent hotel in an ancient olive mill on the edge of the old village. Some 20 tastefully furnished rooms with every comfort (including air conditioning). Sophisticated dishes are served in the elegant, vaulted dining room.

Le Prieuré
Bonnieux
Tel: 4 90 75 80 78
Converted priory with 10 rooms, furnished in a classic style; guests are sometimes received rather formally. There is a restaurant, or eat outside during fine weather.

Sévan
Avenue Verdun
Pertuis
Tel: 4 90 79 35 77
On the road to Manosque, this is a functional rather than cosy hotel with 35 rooms, swimming pool, tennis court. The hotel's restaurant, L'Olivier, is one of the best locally, but not exceptional.

RESTAURANTS

Auberge de la Loube
Buoux
Tel: 4 90 74 19 58
Popular restaurant in a 17th-century farmhouse. Some *hors d'oeuvres* may include 15 dishes; the main courses are traditional Provençal. Also has a car museum. Buoux is between Lourmarin and Apt.

La Fenière
Lourmarin
Tel: 4 90 68 11 79
In the heart of the village. Formally dressed *maître d'hôtel*, stylish interior, softly played jazz music. Inventive, delicious dishes as well as more traditional food such as casseroles etc. The cheapest menu is definitely good value for money.

Le Fournil
Bonnieux
Tel: 4 90 75 83 62
Excellent restaurant with terrace, overlooking a small square in the centre of the village. The menu features carefully prepared mouth-watering regional cuisine.

The hilltop village of Cucuron is dominated by a surprisingly large church, Notre-Dame-de-Beaulieu, while, on the other side of the little square, two towers rise above the roofs: the St-Michel (the only remaining part of a castle which no longer exists) and the Tour de l'Horloge. The small *Musée Marc Deydier* has a collection of archeological objects and local memorabilia.

Ansouis is the next stop, via the D56. You can see its well-preserved château from afar, built on top of the hill against which the village nestles, and surrounded by beautiful terraced gardens. The fortified church of St-Martin dates from the 13th century and the *Musée Extraordinaire* features works of art and marine exotica.

Now take the quiet, narrow road leading to La Tour d'Aigues where you will find the largest wine producer in the Côtes du Lubéron, the Cellier de Marrenon cooperative. Old engravings show that this little agricultural town had a magnificent castle which was first mentioned in the 11th century. The castle was considerably enlarged in the 16th century by Jean-Louis Nicolas de Bouliers who added further pavilions and imposing corner towers. In 1792 the château went up in flames and many of its stones were used to build houses; but the castle has been gradually restored since 1974. The cellars now house two museums: one for ceramics, and one to show the history of the Pays d'Aigues. In summer, performances are given in the inner courtyard as part of the *Festival du Sud Lubéron* (theatre,

Maison Ollier
Lourmarin
Tel: 4 90 68 02 03
Enjoy the Mediterranean dishes
(sometimes with Italian overtones),
served with a smile. Small garden.
Stéphani
Cadenet
Tel: 4 90 68 07 14
Dining room with contemporary
décor and pleasant view. Menu
notable for its à la carte menu based
on fresh, seasonal ingredients.

LOCAL ATTRACTIONS

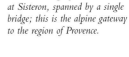

● Pertuis: hosts a cartoon festival in
May and a flower parade every year
on the first weekend in June.
● There are also concerts held
in Lourmarin Castle during July
and August.
● Apt's speciality is candied fruit
(especially cherries). Visit the
Aptunion cooperative for a tasting.
● During the summer months, there
are guided tours through the old
centre of Pertuis every Thursday
morning. For further information,
ask at the *office du tourisme*.
● Three walks have been mapped
out around Cadenet, and four more
around Lourmarin.
● You can also walk (following
a marked path) through a wood
of cedar trees near Bonnieux.

LOCAL MARKETS

● Pertuis holds a daily market.
● Monday is market day in Cadenet.
● Bonnieux has a market on Fridays,
Apt on Saturdays and Cucuron
on Tuesdays.

Left *The mighty River Durance
at Sisteron, spanned by a single
bridge; this is the alpine gateway
to the region of Provence.*

dance and music). The visit to the castle itself is given a
special dimension because of its floor tiles, which produce
musical sounds as you tread.

Follow the D135 from La Tour d'Aigues to Mirabeau to
conclude the Lubéron tour. The castle above the village is
not open to the public. The east and west entrances of the
village are flanked by two fortified towers and the church
has a striking gilt pulpit which is well worth seeing.

COTEAUX DE PIERREVERT

RECOMMENDED PRODUCERS

MANOSQUE
Coopérative
Located on the crossroads to the
south of the town.

GREOUX-LES-BAINS
Château du Rousset
This *domaine* is actually closer to
Manosque than to Gréoux. Take
the D907 in Manosque to cross
the Durance; continue on the D4
south for about 1km. The red wine
produced here is more robust than
average for the region, and a delicious
rosé is also made.

PIERREVERT
Domaine la Blaque
The owner was the first private
wine producer to bottle Coteaux
de Pierrevert. Delicious white and
rosé wines and supple reds. The
estate also uses the name Domaine
du Châteauneuf.
Coopérative
Produces a range of Coteaux de
Pierrevert wines at reasonable prices.
Domaine de Régusse
Dynamic wine-producing estate of
230ha (also produces *vins de pays*
and Côtes du Lubéron). A range
of wines includes a red Cuvée de
Prestige, aged in wood. Also pleasant
vins de pays made with Pinot Noir
and Viognier. The *domaine* has a
tasting and sales outlet just outside
Manosque on the D907.

HOTELS

Hostellerie de la Fuste
La Fuste
Tel: 4 92 72 05 95
The most comfortable hotel in the
region with 15 rooms. Excellent
restaurant with refined, inventive
dishes using the best ingredients.
La Fuste is on the east bank of the
Durance, across from Manosque.

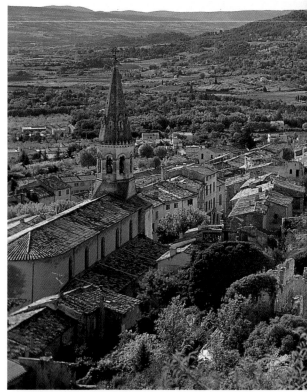

Above *Cucuron is a typical hilltop
Lubéron village rising above vines
used to make white and rosé wines.*

Top *Roman remains litter the
landscape in romantic profusion in
the vicinity of the town of Apt.*

COTEAUX DE PIERREVERT

The wine region of Coteaux de Pierrevert is located immediately to the east of the Côtes du Lubéron. The boundary is not so much physical as administrative, because the wines of Pierrevert are not produced in the Vaucluse but in the Alpes de Haute-Provence; some maintain that these are the highest vineyards in France.

In theory, Coteaux de Pierrevert is a vast region including over 40 villages. It is classified not as an AOC, but a VDQS - *vin délimité de qualité supérieure*. This latter category is less-used today than it was ten years ago as many former VDQS wines have been promoted.

In practice, production is concentrated in three *communes*: Pierrevert, Manosque and Gréoux-les-Bains. The first two are on the hilly, west bank of the Durance

Motel des Quintrands
Manosque
Tel: 4 92 72 08 86
Modern hotel with 20 rooms, swimming pool and restaurant. Located a few kilometres outside the town, on the N96, towards Digne.

RESTAURANT

André
Place du Terreau, Manosque
Tel: 4 92 72 03 09
This restaurant offers sustaining, reasonably priced regional dishes, served in unpretentious but agreeable surroundings. Overlooks the large square in the old centre of the town.

● Guided tour through the town in Manosque every first Tuesday of the month (*office du tourisme,* Place Joubert).
● Manosque holds a general market on the Place du Terreau and a craft market in the Place Magnol, both on Saturday mornings.
● Medieval days are held in Manosque in June every year.
● Pierrevert has an 18-hole golf course (with hotel and restaurant).
● Pierrevert celebrates the feast of its patron saint, St Patrice, at Whitsun.

river and the latter on the east bank. There are some 300 hectares of vineyards in total. The wines are mostly red, but rosé is considered the most successful style, made using Cinsaut, Carignan and Grenache grapes and generally pleasantly tart and fresh on the palate. White wines are made with Clairette, Marsanne and Roussane grapes.

The drive from Mirabeau in the Lubéron along the N96 to Manosque, a lively town of Celtic origin, takes about 20 minutes. The oval-shaped town centre is surrounded by boulevards and has a striking 14th-century town gate on the west side, the Porte Saunerie. In the Rue Grande are the churches of St-Sauveur, with its magnificent bell tower and 17th-century organ and Notre-Dame de Romigier, which has a black Madonna and a fifth-century sarcophagus. Paintings of local interest are exhibited at the town hall.

Follow the road signs to Pierrevert, the wine capital of Coteaux de Pierrevert. This village was built on the slopes of a hill, and has a medieval centre with ruins of gates and walls, and a church portal and chapel dating from the 13th century. Look out for the local wine cooperative at the bottom of the hill, and two wine *domaines* on the road to La Bastide-des-Jourdans; then follow the first unsurfaced road near the Domaine La Blaque and it will take you back to Mirabeau via Beaumont-de-Pertuis.

Above *The Château du Rousset near Manosque, producer of some quality red Coteaux de Pierrevert as well as excellent rosé.*

Right *Evidence of orderly vine management at the large estate of Domaine de Régusse; the wood-aged red wine is unusual and delicious.*

Marseille

HOTELS

New Hôtel Bompard
2 Rue des Flots-Bleus
Tel: 4 91 52 10 93
This is a rarity; a really quiet hotel
in the heart of this busy city, with
a garden, close to the coast road.
It consists of a main building and
various bungalows, 45 rooms in all.
Swimming pool; no restaurant.

St Ferréol's Hôtel
19 Rue Pisançon
Tel: 4 91 33 12 21
A small centrally located hotel,
simple yet comfortable, with 20
rooms. Located in a pedestrianised
street within easy walking distance
of the Old Port.

RESTAURANTS

Le Caribou
38 Place Thiars
Tel: 4 91 33 22 63
A friendly and relaxed establishment
near the old port, which features
excellent *fruits de mer* (seafood).
Reasonable prices.

Marimar
12 Quai du Port
Tel: 4 91 91 10 40
Michelin-starred restaurant. Noted
for seafood and for excellent
examples of regional cuisine, such
as *bouillabaisse,* and also *bourride*,
a creamy fish soup made with
monkfish and lashings of garlic.

Surely you mean Marseilles? The spelling confusion is the first of many about this notorious city, the second largest in France and chiefly renowned internationally for its gangster history, sinister connections with the drugs trade and for the invention of *pastis* in its many forms, that quintessentially French café drink.

For many visitors to Provence this is the first (forgive the pun) port of call and it is a pity to waste the opportunity to look around before embarking on that first wine tasting. Though not immediately glamorous or charming, with its bleak 1960s housing estates and industrial emphasis, Marseille (the French spelling) repays effort to discover its historic buildings and also some superb cuisine in its restaurants. One of the fascinations of the place is its air of business, of purpose and hard work. The locals pride themselves in being characters, extrovert and weatherbeaten Mediterranean types, like those immortalised in the much-filmed novels of local writer Marcel Pagnol.

Right *Notre-Dame-de-la-Garde;*
the basilica dates from the 2nd
Empire period and is crowned with a
golden statue of the Virgin.
Far right *Fortresses guard the*
entrance to Marseille's Vieux Port.

Above *The charm of a traditional fishing harbour still at Vallon des Auffes, tucked away below the city on the Malmousque peninsula.*

The main thoroughfare of the city is La Canabière which begins at the head of the Vieux Port; this is also the location of the tourist office. The name of the road derives from the word *chènevrières*, referring to the hemp fields which once grew locally to supply rope for ships. Standing here you are a part of local history, which stretches back to the arrival of the first Greek sailors in ancient times, through Romans to invading Germans in the Second World War. The harbour entrance is guarded by twin fortresses, one commissioned by Louis XIV, the Sun King, as a symbol of his subjugation of the city. Provence has historically viewed itself as separate from the court in Paris, and even retains vestiges of its old local language today.

Escaping the busy traffic of the port, there are plenty of lively quayside cafés in the pedestrianized streets between this part of the quay and the Cours Etienne d'Orves a few streets south. This is a popular area to stroll and be seen for the locals, a reminder that Marseille is not really a tourist resort but a working city. The fish market on the quayside is another good place to watch the Marseillaise people in action and to be amazed at the variety and eccentricity of the fish on sale.

Many will be destined for *bouillabaisse*, and sampling a bowl while in the city should be obligatory. This saffron and garlic-scented fish soup has a wide variety of recipes and styles, but it is almost always accompanied by delicious croutons and a spicy relish known as *rouille*.

For those who prefer meat, the other local delicacy is *pieds et paquets*, a rich combination of lamb belly and pigs' trotters. These dishes are available in many small restaurants around the old port.

WHAT TO SEE IN THE CITY

Apart from the lively old port area, there is a remarkably stylish beach esplanade known as the Corniche Avenue J-F-Kennedy, ideal for strolling and admiring some fine coastal views as well as villas on the slopes above. It is fun to walk here at night and admire the array of restaurants and night clubs, as well as the smart houses in Malmousque, a fashionable residential district on an unspoilt peninsula. From here it would be possible to continue on all the way to the harbour village of Cassis (*see* page 101) for a well-deserved glass of the excellent local white wine.

Before leaving Marseille, there are some fine churches which are worth a visit, including the basilica of St-Victor, founded in the fifth century and more like a fortified castle than a church, and the Hospice de la Vielle Charité, a 17th-century workhouse with a fine Baroque chapel and an impressive museum that houses a collection devoted to Mediterranean archeology.

This is sited in the working-class district of Le Panier, an area of many bitter memories for locals, after the old quarter was burned to the ground by the Nazis during the Second World War occupation of France.

On a lighter note, the markets of Marseille are a riot of life, with everything from cooked meats to cheap clothes and plenty of haggling for goods. The Sunday morning flea market is a great show at the Avenue du Cap-Pinède. Smart shops and specialist markets for stamp collectors or rare book enthusiasts may be found on the cours Julien, south-east of the old port near the place Paul Cézanne. This is also an area for late-night restaurants and cafés. From Marseille, either take the D559 towards Cassis and Bandol, or head north along the N8 to start a tour from Aix-en-Provence.

Above Quintessential Marseille: the early-morning fishing catch at the Marché aux Poissons, on the Quai des Belges beside the Vieux Port.

Coteaux Varois

Coteaux Varois is an inland area bordered to the south, west and east by Côtes de Provence. This region waited 20 years for its *appellation contrôlée* and it was finally successful in March 1993. Unfortunately only 28 of the 41 nominated *communes* could share the celebrations as the remainder were situated too high in altitude and were therefore ineligible for the AOC.

There is a small enclave of Coteaux Varois, (the villages of Salernes and Villecroze), in the Côtes de Provence wine region. For many years Villecroze has produced an excellent Coteaux Varois; a Franco-American couple were early pioneers here. Some writers have hailed this part of France as the 'new California' because of its benevolent climate and vast potential for good-quality wine. As in Côtes de Provence the majority of the wine produced is rosé: 65 per cent in fact, with 30 per cent red and five per cent white.

Most red Coteaux Varois should be drunk young; the wines have a round, supple taste with a hint of red berries and spice. Grenache, Syrah and Mourvèdre are the main grape varieties used: by the year 2000 at least two of these varieties must make up 80 per cent of any wine's composition. Cooperatives are the largest producers, but private domaines produce the best wines, and some of the top producers are to be found in the villages described in the following pages.

TOURING THE COTEAUX VAROIS

The route for the Coteaux Varois wine region starts in Tourves, a village slightly to the east of St-Maximin-la-Ste-Baume and Nans-les-Pins. Tourves used to be a famous road-traffic bottleneck because it was the point where two *routes nationales* converged. Fortunately that situation has now been eased by a bypass and traces of the town's Roman

Left *Fresh water and shade for the weary traveller visiting the former industrial town of Brignoles.*

Above *A pleasant environment to taste some good local rosé wines: the Château de Fontainebleau, Le Val.*

Coteaux Varois

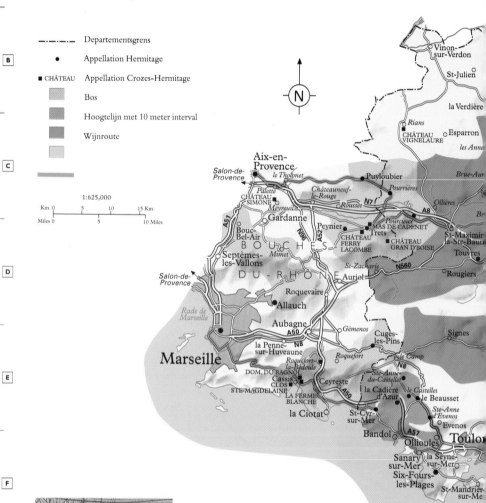

- —·—·—· Departementsgrens
- • Appellation Hermitage
- ■ CHÂTEAU Appellation Crozes-Hermitage
- Bos
- Hoogtelijn met 10 meter interval
- Wijnroute

1:625,000

Km. 0   5   10   15 Km.
Miles 0   5   10 Miles

N

Vinon-sur-Verdon
St-Julien
la Verdière
Rians
CHÂTEAU VIGNELAURE   Esparron
les Anne
Aix-en-Provence
Salon-de-Provence
le Tholonet
Puyloubier
Brue-Au
Châteauneuf-le-Rouge
Pourrières
Palette
CHÂTEAU SIMONE
Meyreuil
Rousset
N7
Ollières
A8
Br
Gardanne
Peynier
Pourcieux
MAS DE CADENET
Bouc-Bel-Air
B O U C H E S
A52
N96
Trets
St-Maximir la-Ste-Baun
CHÂTEAU FERRY LACOMBE
CHÂTEAU GRAN D'BOISE
Septèmes-les-Vallons
Mimet
D U   R H O N E
St-Zacharie
N560
Touvres
Rougiers
Salon-de-Provence
Auriol
Roquevaire
Allauch
Rade de Marseille
Aubagne
A50
Gémenos
Cuges-les-Pins
Signes
Marseille
la Penne-sur-Huveaune
N8
Roquefort
le Camp
Roquefort-la-Bédoule
N8
DOM. DU BAGNOL
Cassis
CLOS
STE-MAGDELAINE
LA FERME BLANCHE
Ceyreste
Ste-Anne-du-Castellet
A50
la Cadière d'Azur
le Castellet
le Beausset
Ste-Anne d'Evenos
la Ciotat
St-Cyr-sur-Mer
Evenos
Bandol
A57
Ollioules
Toulor
Sanary-sur-Mer
la Seyne-sur-Mer
Six-Fours-les-Plages
St-Mandrier-sur-Me

Above *After the steep climb to the village of La Celle, recuperate in a café with a glass of local wine.*

origins can be appreciated quietly once more in Tourves' steep, narrow streets. The most important and interesting building is the local castle, the Château de Valbelle, which is only accessible on foot. It dates originally from the Middle Ages but was extensively renovated and enlarged in the 18th century to make it one of the most impressive châteaux in Provence. The entrance is marked by an obelisk 24 metres high, a copy of a Roman original. The oldest part of this semi-ruined castle lies behind an enormous colonnade. The surrounding park was once magnificent but today it is sadly overgrown and only traces of its former glory remain.

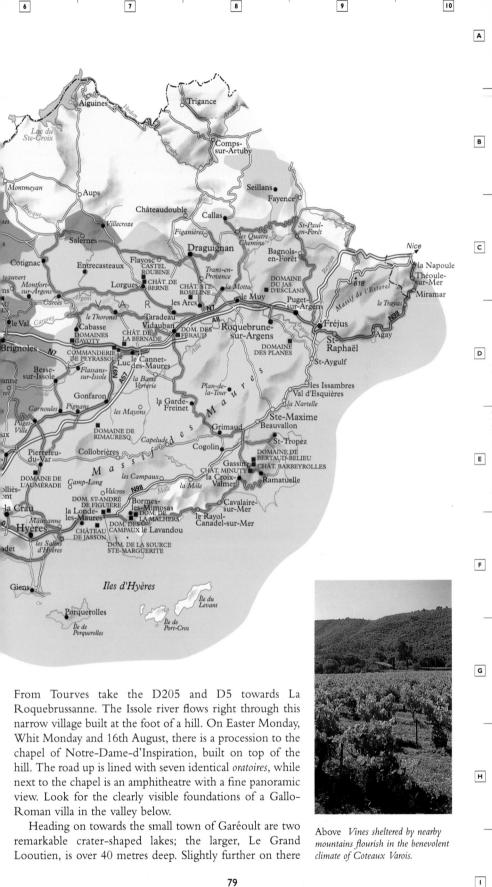

Aiguines

Trigance

Lac du
Ste-Croix

Comps-
sur-Artuby

Montmeyan

Aups

Seillans

Fayence

Châteaudouble

Callas

Villecroze

Figanières

St-Paul-
en-Forêt

Salernes

les Quatre
Chemins

Nice

Cotignac

Draguignan

Bagnols-
en-Forêt

la Napoule

Entrecasteaux

Flayosc
CASTEL
ROUBINE

Trans-en-
Provence

Théoule-
sur-Mer

teauvert
Montfort-
sur-Argens

Lorgues

CHÂT. DE
BERNE

CHÂT. STE-
ROSELINE

la Motte

DOMAINE
DU JAS
D'ESCLANS

618

Miramar

Carcès

V A R

les Arcs

N7

le Muy

Puget-
sur-Argens

Massif de l'Esterel

le Trayas

le Val

le Thoronet

Taradeau
Vidauban

A8

Roquebrune-
sur-Argens

Fréjus

Agay

Cabasse
DOMAINES
GAVOTY

CHÂT. DE
LA BERNADE

DOM. DES
FÉRAUD

DOMAINE
DES PLANES

St
Raphaël

Brignoles

N7

COMMANDERIE
DE PEYRASSOL

le
Luc

le Cannet-
des-Maures

St-Aygulf

Besse-
sur-Issole

Flassans-
sur-Issole

la Basse
Verrerie

les Issambres
Val d'Esquières

anne

Gonfaron

Plan-de-
la-Tour

la Nartelle

Carnoules

Pignans

les Mayons

la Garde-
Freinet

Ste-Maxime

Puget-
Ville

DOMAINE DE
RIMAURESQ

Capelude

Grimaud

Beauvallon

Cogolin

St-Tropez

Pierrefeu-
du-Var

Collobrières

les Campaux

DOMAINE DE
BERTAUD-BELIEU

CHÂT. BARBEYROLLES

DOMAINE DE
L'AUMÉRADE

Camp-Long

Gassin
CHÂT. MINUTY
la Croix-
Valmer

Ramatuelle

la Crau

DOM. ST-ANDRÉ
DE FIGUIÈRE

Valcros

la Môle

olliès-
ont

Bormes-
les-Mimosas

Cavalaire-
sur-Mer

Hyères

la Londe-
les-Maures

DOM. DE
LA MALHERS

le Rayol-
Canadel-sur-Mer

CHÂTEAU
DE JASSON

DOM. DES
CAMPAUX le Lavandou

les Salins
d'Hyères

DOM. DE LA SOURCE
STE-MARGUERITE

Giens

Iles d'Hyères

Île du
Levant

Porquerolles

Île de
Porquerolles

Île de
Port-Cros

From Tourves take the D205 and D5 towards La Roquebrussanne. The Issole river flows right through this narrow village built at the foot of a hill. On Easter Monday, Whit Monday and 16th August, there is a procession to the chapel of Notre-Dame-d'Inspiration, built on top of the hill. The road up is lined with seven identical *oratoires*, while next to the chapel is an amphitheatre with a fine panoramic view. Look for the clearly visible foundations of a Gallo-Roman villa in the valley below.

Heading on towards the small town of Garéoult are two remarkable crater-shaped lakes; the larger, Le Grand Looutien, is over 40 metres deep. Slightly further on there

Above Vines sheltered by nearby mountains flourish in the benevolent climate of Coteaux Varois.

Above *Barjols was once a centre for the tanning industry and there is still a curious festival held here each January, when a cow is killed and roasted in honour of St Marcel.*

Right *A glorious setting for vines near La Celle; the fresh-tasting wines made under this youthful appellation (awarded in March 1993) repay early drinking.*

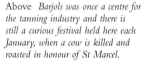

COTEAUX VAROIS

RECOMMENDED PRODUCERS

Some producers also produce Côtes de Provence and *vins de pays* as well as Coteaux Varois.

TOURVES
Domaine de Boulon
Large operation making good rosé.

LA ROQUEBRUSSANNE
Domaine du Loou
A good range of reliable wines from a leading wine-producing *domaine* on an ancient Roman site. The red Cuvée Spéciale is a successful combination of Syrah, Grenache and Mourvèdre. The Clos des Blaquières is slightly more supple. A juicy *vin de pays* is made with 100% Cabernet Sauvignon. There are ruins of a Gallo-Roman villa in the *domaine*.

GAREOULT
Domaine des Chaberts
Hospitable wine estate, with cellars, a rather modern villa and an attractive hillside setting. Particularly recommended are the red Cuvée Prestige, rich and tannic, and the rosé Cuvée Spéciale; it also produces some pleasant white wines.

are signs to the Domaine des Chaberts, a leading Coteaux Varois estate. The best day to visit Garéoult is Tuesday for the weekly market in the town centre.

The next wine village is Forcalqueiret, named after the lime kilns it once had. On a hill slightly to the south are the impressive ruins of a vast 16th-century castle, known locally as Le Castellas. Just before Brignoles, which is on the D554, look for a turning leading to the hilltop village of La Celle, which is well worth visiting. The royal abbey there is one of the oldest in Provence, dating from the sixth century. Visit the Maison des Coteaux Varois at the abbey for local wine information .

Brignoles is a busy, noisy country town, and it also suffers from its proximity to the N7. To visit the old town, once surrounded by walls, park the car and walk to the Place des Comtes de Provence. The former palace of the Counts of Provence is one of the few surviving 13th-century secular buildings in Provence. Today it has become a museum displaying local artefacts including a model bauxite mine, a typical Provençal kitchen, and paintings by local artists. For a fine view of the old quarter climb the tower of the St-Louis chapel, which also houses an impressive collection of religious art. Other buildings of interest include a former Royal Prison, next to the palace, and the medieval church of St-Sauveur in the town centre. If you leave Brignoles on the notorious N7, signs appear to

'Mini France'. This pleasure ground should appeal to model-makers or younger members of the family; it covers an area of two hectares, laid out in the shape of France, with miniatures of famous buildings and monuments, including the châteaux of the Loire.

Otherwise, take the road northward to Le Val. As the name suggests, it lies in a valley which can be reached by a tortuous stretch of the D554. That Le Val is a wine village is obvious from by the large mural on the façade of the Hôtel des Vins. Local wine and olive producers both sell their wares here. There is plenty to see in Le Val. The *Musée des Santons* has an large collection of painted figurines, traditional to Provence since the days of Napoleon, as well as Christmas cribs from Spain, Italy, Brazil and the Ivory Coast. The museum is housed in a communal bakery which dates back to the 12th century. Near the churchyard is the chapel of L'Annonciade which now houses the *Musée de l'Art Sacré*.

From Le Val, take the D552 and follow signs for Montfort-sur-Argens. On the way you will drive past the Château de Fontainebleau where excellent wines are produced. Rather unromantically, Montfort is celebrated as the birthplace of Jean-Louis Lambot who invented reinforced concrete. The house where he lived is down in the old village. Although the local castle is not open to visitors, the old town is pleasant to visit, with picturesque,

Domaine de Garbelle
Good rosé and heavy, balsamic red wine with a complex flavour.

LA CELLE
Domaine de la Gayolle
Probably more interesting for its location than its wines: the Chapelle de la Gayolle is on the property, where several sarcophagi have been discovered. The most famous, named after the domaine, can be seen in the *Musée du Pays Brignolais* in Brignoles.

BRIGNOLES
Domaine de Ramatuelle
Situated on the road to Bras. Delicious red wines, rich in berry aromas, and refreshing, lively rosés.

LE VAL
Château de Fontainebleau
Attractive old estate with a fine fountain, making full-bodied rosés.
Château Réal Martin
Their red wines are only sold after maturing for two years. The domaine is on the D28 towards Bras.

CHATEAUVERT
Château Routas
Pleasant and fruity red wines. The Cuvée Pyranus white is wood-aged.

BRUE-AURIAC
Château St-Estève
Produce a range of wines including
red wood-aged Coteaux Varois
and a powerful, heavy rosé.

BRAS
Domaine des Annibals
Situated on the road to Brignoles
producing an attractive rosé,
Vin des Roches, and also an
agreeable white Coteaux Varois.
Domaine de Clapiers
Their red wine is meaty and rustic,
ideal to accompany rich, oily, garlic-
scented Provençal dishes.

NEOULES
Domaine de Trians
Spicy, fruity red wine.

Above *The charm of Brignole's
medieval quarter contrasts with its
history as a centre for the mining of
bauxite, used to produce aluminium.*

Top right *Brignoles is the major
town in Coteaux Varois; it hosts
an important wine fair each April,
for all the wines of Provence.*

Right *Tucked away in a hidden
valley, Le Val has several interesting
churches and museums as well as
this mural on the Hôtel des Vins
celebrating its vinous history.*

narrow streets and fountains, a 13th-century gate and a fine
bell tower. The road to Correns, the next village, runs
through the valley of the River Argens with fine vineyard
views. This is the meeting point of the Coteaux Varois and
Côtes de Provence appellations.

In Correns itself the wine cooperative is located next to
an ancient bridge. In front of the surprisingly large, 18th-
century village church is a wine press. Each May, a
procession passes through the *porte du pardon* of the church
and tours the village, offering sinners forgiveness for their
misdeeds of the year.

Continue along a designated scenic route as the D45
runs through a picturesque ravine to the hamlet of
Châteauvert. Follow the D554 north to Barjols and admire

WINE COMPETITION

During Brignoles agricultural fair (April 1-10), a competition is organised for all Provence wines.

HOTELS

Château de Brignoles-en-Provence
Brignoles
Tel: 4 94 69 06 88
Family-run hotel with around 40 rooms, most of them very comfortable. Large garden, tennis court, swimming pool. Restaurant serving simple Provençal food. On Avenue Dréo (N7, direction Nice); so ask for a room at the back.

Auberge la Loube
La Roquebrussanne
Tel: 4 94 86 81 36
Pretty, light rooms, eight in all. The hotel was completely renovated in 1993. Modern comforts and small, neat bathrooms. A homely dining room serves traditional dishes.

Le Pont d'Or
Barjols
Tel: 4 94 77 05 23
Simple rooms (16), some of which have a view of the valley. Unpretentious restaurant. The cheese platter often includes *Tomme de Barjols*, a fresh goats' cheese.

RESTAURANTS

La Fontaine
Le Val
Tel: 4 94 86 32 32
Excellent reputation for seafood (including *bouillabaisse*) but also serves *foie gras* and meat dishes from the grill.

A la Fortune du Pot
St-Estève (near Brue-Auriac)
Tel: 4 94 80 90 83
Simple inn (with rooms) serving affordable cuisine, local wines.

LOCAL MARKETS

- Flea market every second Sunday of the month in Brignoles (Place Carami, or in the covered market on rainy days, in the centre of town).
- The annual *Foire à la Saucisse* (Sausage Fair) takes place in Le Val at the beginning of September.
- A pottery fair is held in Barjols around 20th July each year.
- Local market days include: Tourves on Tuesday; Garéoult on Tuesday; Brignoles on Saturday; Barjols on Tuesday and Thursday; Bras on Sunday and Wednesday.

the dramatic preview of the village, with its terraces on a chalk hillside and the ruins of a castle that was built in the 12th century. In the past this 'Tivoli of Provence' was well known for its tanning trade, but nowadays it is renowned for its numerous fountains (about 30 in all). Village life is centred around the large Place de la Rougière, narrow at one end and wide at the other. The 11th-century Notre-Dame-des-Epines church has some beautiful furniture inside, while the nearby Hôtel des Pontèves has a strikingly attractive façade. The oldest part of the town is known as the Quartier du Réal.

Brue-Auriac is a village in the heart of the Coteaux Varois. From Barjols, the road winds sharply through dramatic landscape towards the source of the River Argens. As you arrive in the village, look out for the tallest dovecote in Europe (built in 1750). Note also the elegant central *cours* in the village, constructed by order of Georges de Roux, a wealthy merchant who wanted to create a special quarter for local farmers and workers.

The final leg of this journey will take you on to Bras, via the D35, but first stop at the hamlet of St-Estève where you will find not only a wine domaine but also a ceramic workshop and a restaurant. From here, a narrow, green lane leads to Bras where the ruins of an older village and chapel may be seen on a hilltop; just the spot for a picnic with fine panoramic views.

Bras is the final point of this tour round Coteaux Varois. The next chapter starts in Flassans-sur-Issole which is reached via Le Val, Brignoles and the eastbound N7.

Côtes de Provence

Côtes de Provence is by far the largest wine region in Provence. It covers approximately 18,000 hectares, spread over three *départements,* with 15 villages in the Bouches-du-Rhône (*see* the chapter on the Palette area, page 55), one in the Alpes-Maritimes (*see* Bellet, page 125) and 48 in the Var. The mountains of the Massif des Maures run right through the wine region; the soil varies widely near these mountains, ranging from clay and sand to calcareous, gravel and clay, sometimes with schist and granite. Scenically, the landscape is also varied, as flat plateaux give way to slopes covered with terraced vines. There are also areas with their own microclimate. Natural factors alone account for the great variety in the wines.

Human factors, such as the choice of grape varieties, the moment chosen to pick the grapes, and the various stages of making the wine further underline these differences.

This variety makes wine tasting here an exciting event, especially when sampling red and white wines. Many reds include some Syrah in the blend for added bite and keeping quality. The rosés are slightly less varied; they are always dry, often with a slight orangey tint and a fairly robust taste. Côtes de Provence rosé is an ideal summer wine to reflect the Provençal lifestyle and cuisine; this style of wine accounts for three-quarters of the production and is the most widely available *appellation contrôlée* rosé in the world. Locally, it makes an ideal accompaniment for dishes like *soupe au pistou* or *bouillabaisse.*

Wines and villages within the region of Côtes de Provence are described in the following pages and also in the sections Fréjus and the eastern Côtes de Provence (*see* page 95), Palette and the western Côtes de Provence (*see* page 55), in the chapter including Bandol (*see* page 104), and around Bellet (*see* page 125).

Left Some of the best Côtes de Provence wines are made here in the Var, in the area around Taradeau.

Above The cliffs above Villecroze have been furrowed by caves and chasms over the course of centuries.

Above *Château de Selle at Taradeau is synonymous with the Ott brothers who have done much to raise the profile of Provençal wines.*

COTES DE PROVENCE

RECOMMENDED PRODUCERS

FLASSANS-SUR-ISOLE
Château Payan
Excellent red Cuvée Leopold, with rich berry flavour; also Cuvée Fanny, a highly rated rosé wine.
Commanderie de Peyrassol
Named after the Knights Templar. Try the red Cuvée Marie-Estelle under the Château de Peyrassol label or the rosé Cuvée d'Art under the Commanderie label. Quality rosé is the speciality of the estate.
Domaine de St-Baillon
The red Cuvée is a blend of Cabernet Sauvignon and Syrah, aged in wood. White and rosé Cuvée Opale. Also produce Coteaux Varois.

BESSE-SUR-ISSOLE
Domaine de Cabasson
Established in a 17th-century *bastide*.

GONFARON
Domaine de Beaumet
The fresh, floral-scented white wine made here is highly recommended.
Domaine de l'Esparron
Their rosé has strawberry aromas and is deliciously refreshing to drink.

LE LUC
Bastide de Bertrands
Classic style white wines, tasting like Sémillon, although produced from other local varieties. Also notable for some other red wines including Cabernet Sauvignon.

IN THE HEART OF THE VAR

The trip described below can easily take a couple of days because of the many interesting sights and wine *domaines* scattered along the way. Almost every *commune* visited belongs to the Côtes de Provence *appellation contrôlée*, but a couple in the north, Villecroze and Salernes, produce Coteaux Varois. Start your journey in Flassans-sur-Issole, an attractive village with a ruined castle, set close to the main N7 road. Follow the River Issole along the D13 southwest to Besse-sur-Issole; note the prolific vineyards on either side.

Continue on the D13 and N97 to Gonfaron, the southernmost village on this route. Relax here for a while in the pretty square with ancient plane trees providing welcome shade. In the past, the village was famous for its cork industry. Now people come from far and wide to Gonfaron for L'Hermitage bakery, which is especially renowned for its delicious olive bread.

Continue on the N97 to Le Luc; a village sadly over-shadowed by motorway flyovers, but still notable for its wine and olive production. On the south side of the village is an eye-catching three-storey hexagonal tower, dating from 1517. Philatelists will be able to feast their eyes on the stamp collections at the *Musée Régional du Timbre et de Philatélie* in the 18th-century Château des Vintimille. Le Luc also has a museum devoted to the history of the region; the *Musée Historique du Centre Var*, located in the Chapelle Ste-Anne.

For an overview of the area, look for signs to Le Vieux Cannet; this hill village has some fine old buildings, including a Romanesque church with a clock tower. Admire the scene below before returning to Le Luc, then taking the D33 to Cabasse, in the Issole Valley. The church of St-Pons (15th century) has a magnificent altarpiece. There are several dolmens and traces of Gallo-Roman architecture near the village, including a bridge.

Continue on the D13 and D79 towards the Abbey of Le Thoronet. *En route* you will spot a large bauxite mine, one of many in the area and a reminder of another source of revenue locally. Le Thoronet itself is a perfect example of Cistercian architecture, dating in part from the 12th century. The neighbouring hamlet of Le Thoronet is just a few shady streets, but there is a wine connection. This was

Above Substantial vine cultivation in the AOC Côtes de Provence area reflects the success of this appellation internationally.

Bastide de la Bernarde
Large, successful *domaine* which
was one of the first to produce
good, red Côtes de Provence.
Delicious red Clos Bernarde.

Domaine de Brique
Cellars at the foot of a hexagonal
tower. Associated with nearby
Château les Meyans.

Domaine de la Lauzade
Built on the site of an early Roman
villa; here they make very fruity red
wine, and also white wine with a
fruity flavour from Sémillon.

LE CANNET-DES-MAURES

Château Reillane
Makes an excellent example of the
local rosé; pale in colour but full of
delicacy and style on the palate.

Château de Roux
The red wine is spicy and has a
blackcurrant flavour; it repays keeping.

Domaine de la Bastide Neuve
Notable red and rosé wines are
made here; well-balanced and classy.
Liquorice and vanilla tones may be
found in the red wines..

CABASSE

Domaines Gavoty
Wines made by a musical family with
a great emphasis on quality. The
Cuvée Clarendon rosé and white
wines are excellent; the red wines are
also good but not outstanding. There
is a farm shop for local produce.

Domaine des Pomples
Good for lively, fruity rosé wines.

LE THORONET

Domaine de l'Abbaye
Delicious wines, including the fruity
rosé Clos Beylesse in a blue bottle,
and the red Cuvée Pugette.

VIDAUBAN

Château d'Astros
This was a *commanderie* for the
Knights Templar, noted today for
its red wines; also makes white
wines from 100% Rolle.

Coopérative
Try the red Roubertas.

Domaine de Féraud
Excellent red, rosé and white wines,
including the red Cuvée Antiopolis.
Also sells wines under the name
Domaine de Peissonel.

Right *Steep-sided cliffs and gorges
area a feature of the area.*
Top right *A plethora of vineyards
surround the River Issole; the grapes
are vinified by domaines and also in
cooperatives, mainly as rosé.*

home to Victor Ganzin, the man who discovered the vine weevil phylloxera. He was also a pioneer in the field of crossing grape varieties.

The valley of the Argens and the D84 lead to Vidauban whose name is derived from *Vitis Alba*, Latin for 'white vinestock'. All the traffic of the N7 has to squeeze through the narrow main street of Vidauban whose main redeeming feature is a fountain with gilded lions. On the north side of town, on the D48, look for the monumental wrought iron gates of the Château d'Astros. This castle, reached by a side road, is surrounded by a large park, has some beautiful antique furnture – and makes delicious wines.

Continue on through Taradeau, which has a Romanesque chapel. Driving on and into Lorgues, the eye is caught by a large basilica, much the same size as that of St-Maximin-la-Ste-Baume.

The main street, Boulevard de la République, is picturesque with magnificent plane trees on both sides. Walking along the narrow, shady streets in the old centre of the town you come across quiet little squares, old town gates, fountains, a chapel and a 17th-century clock tower. This pretty little town is surrounded by vineyards and olive trees. Some of the wine estates you pass on the narrow road

TARADEAU

Château Rasque
Remarkable white Côtes de Provence made from Rolle with a rich scent of bananas and exotic fruit. Also makes a fine, meaty red: Cuvée Pièce Noble.

Château de Selle
One of several wine estates belonging to the Ott family, who originally came from Alsace. They have made a great contribution to raising the status of the Côtes de Provence *appellation contrôlée*. Try the complex, truffle-scented red wines which are meant to be aged for several years.

LORGUES

Château de Berne
A large site with Roman origins; also noted for the château's stained glass windows. The rosé wines are stylish and fresh, and the white wines floral-scented and good; the red wines can be rather hard.

Château Mentone
Rather rounded red wines; rosés with a hint of cassis.

Domaine de Castel Roubine
Striking forest location and classy wines, including the red, rosé and white Comte de Bargemon.

CARCES

Domaine St-Eloi
Harmonious rosé, fresh and elegant.

Domaine St-Jean
Commended for its white wine, produced from Rolle and a lively rosé.

COTIGNAC

Château Carpe Diem
'Seize the day' and try the fine white wine with its exotic fruit aromas and good finish.

VILLECROZE

Château Thuerry
Produces both Côtes de Provence and Coteaux Varois.

Domaine St-Jean de Villecroze
Delicious wines made here (Coteaux Varois and Vin de Pays du Var), including a quality Cabernet Sauvignon and Syrah blend, the red Cuvée Spéciale (berry aroma, mostly Cabernet) and the attractive rosé produced from Cinsaut.

FLAYOSC

Domaine de Matourne
Try the red Cuvée de la Tour.

DRAGUIGNAN

Domaine Rabiega
Belongs to the Swedish State Wine & Spirit Monopoly; elegant reception area. One of the best wine estates in Provence, thanks to wines such as the red, blackcurrant-scented Clos d'Ières, which includes a proportion of Syrah.'

LES ARCS-SUR-ARGENS

Château Clarettes
Produces an elegant and refreshing
rosé with a good finish.

Château St-Pierre
These white wines are sometimes
wood-aged and as a result have a
rich, creamy quality in the mouth.

Château Ste-Roseline
Near the famous chapel; has its
own 13th-century cloister. One of
its best wines is the red Réserve,
in a distinctive bottle.

Domaine des Hauts de St-Jean
The soil here is volcanic in origin
giving these bright pink wines an
interesting, complex flavour.

WINE FAIR

● Draguignan holds a wine fair in
August and a *Salon des Vins et Tables
de Provence* in November.

HOTELS

Auberge St-Pierre
Tourtour
Tel: 4 94 70 57 17
Country inn with 20 neat, rustic
rooms. In a 16th-century building
situated on a 70ha estate. Tennis
courts, swimming pool, horse riding,
fishing. Restaurant with sophisticated
regional dishes.

La Bastide de Tourtour
Tourtour
Tel: 4 94 70 57 30
Luxury establishment (Relais et
Châteaux) with 25 stylishly furnished
rooms of various sizes and with
different views. Excellent restaurant.
Terrace, swimming pool, tennis court,
fitness suite, billiard room.

Au Bien-Etre
Villecroze
Tel: 4 94 70 67 57
Eight simple hotel rooms in a peaceful
setting. The restaurant is more classy,
but choose traditional dishes rather
than the unusual combinations on
offer. Small swimming pool.
Friendly reception.

Château les Lonnes
Vidauban
Tel: 4 94 73 65 76
Magnificently restored bastide
surrounded by 22ha of parkland.
A dozen comfortable rooms plus
two suites. Extremely peaceful.
Swimming pool with large terrace.
Monthly wine tasting in the cellars.
No restaurant but the hotel organises
a *route gastronomique* to nearby
restaurants for their guests.

leading to St-Antonin-du-Var are enclosed by walls.
Continue along the tortuous D50 to Entrecasteaux. The
rectangular castle which dominates this village was bought
in 1974 by the Scottish family McGarvie-Munn and they
have restored it with great care and excellent taste. The
castle has an old Provençal kitchen; the gardens were
designed by Le Nôtre.

Carcès, a few kilometres to the south, is located at the
confluence of the Argens and Carami, and has a large lake.
The village was built around a castle, but only a few of its
gates and steps remain.

The next part of the route, from Carcès to Cotignac, is
notable for picturesque vineyards on both sides of the road.
Cotignac, nestling at the foot of an 80-metre tufa wall with
two medieval dungeons at the top, is a romantic place. The
village has a large, oval *cours* shaded by plane trees and with
a marble fountain.

Those searching for a real sense of medieval history
should visit Tourtour, the 'village in the sky'. High on this
hill the Moorish invaders of France staged their last stand.
Just off the pleasant Place des Ormeaux is a small *quartier*
with interesting buildings such as old olive mills and a
fossil museum. The *mairie* and the post office are in an old

Left *Draguignan has a fine medieval quarter as well as threeo interesting museums.*
Far left *Walking in the Gorges du Verdon is not recommended without a professional guide to lead the way.*

Hôtel les Etoiles de l'Ange
Draguignan
Tel: 4 94 68 23 01
Situated on a hill above the town, on the road to Flayosc. Pretty rooms furnished in quite a neutral style, all of them with a balcony and view. Modern comfort. Pleasant restaurant which always has fresh fish. Cheaper lunch menu is served in the terrace room. Small swimming pool.

La Grillade au Feu de Bois
Flassans-sur-Issole
Tel: 4 94 69 71 20
Given the hotel's name, this is a surprisingly stylish establishment: it has 16 pleasant rooms, all with spacious bathrooms. The country restaurant serves delicious dishes from the grill (such as *côtes d'agneau*). The hotel has a swimming pool. Close to the N7 (in the direction of Le Luc) but quiet all the same.

Hôtellerie du Golf de Barbaroux
Flassans-sur-Issole
Tel: 4 94 69 18 00
This establishment has 23 pleasant rooms. The restaurant serves salads, sandwiches and a also offers a reasonably priced menu.

Le Logis du Guetteur
Les Arcs-sur-Argens
Tel: 4 94 73 30 82
Ten rooms in an attractive old castle, all with a view. The restaurant is in a vaulted hall; it serves delicious food such as *pigeon aux truffes* (pigeon with truffles).

Lou Calen
Cotignac
Tel: 4 94 04 60 40
Not sufficiently insulated against sound, but a charming village inn all the same, with 15 rooms. Garden, terrace, swimming pool, restaurant.

Le Mas des Collines
Tourtour
Tel: 4 94 70 59 30
Small hotel with seven rooms, on the road to Villecroze. Attractive hilly setting. The owner does the cooking for the restaurant. Regional cuisine and, in season, many game dishes. Swimming pool.

La Petite Auberge
Tourtour
Tel: 4 94 70 57 16
Situated on a woody hillside in the direction of Flayosc. Very peaceful location: this is a *Relais de Silence*. Eleven simple rooms. Swimming pool.

château. Just outside the village are the church of St-Denis, the square 12th century Tour du Grimaud and the local *bastide* (now a luxury hotel).

Take the D557 from Tourtour to Flayosc. Happily, this is a picturesque, winding road which leads through enchanting wooded hills. Flayosc is a typical Provençal village, built on top of a hill, dominated by a large church with a massive tower. Life in Flayosc is centred around two squares, situated on either side of the main street. Away from the traffic is the very charming Place de la Reinesse with a fountain and a public washhouse. Naturally, Flayosc also has its own wine cooperative and a *cours* devoted to the ubiquitous *jeu de boules*.

The largest town on this itinerary is Draguignan with over 30,000 inhabitants. The Tour de l'Horloge, a clock tower almost 20 metres high, rises dramatically from the bare rock in the town centre. It is surrounded by a network of narrow little streets and squares, including the Place du Marché, where there is a market on Wednesday and Saturday. Note the distinguished buildings along the Grand'Rue and the Rue de l'Observance. There are three museums in Draguignan; the *Musée des Arts et Traditions Populaires*; the *Musée Municipal* for paintings; and southeast on the D59 is the *Musée du Canon et d'Artillerie*.

La Vieille Bastide
Flayosc
Tel: 4 94 70 40 57
Old building, located slightly away
from the centre. Seven recently
renovated rooms. Swimming pool.
Half board is obligatory during July
and August. Fairly large dining-room
on two floors.

RESTAURANTS

Auberge des Lavandes
Villecroze
Tel: 4 94 70 76 00
Friendly restaurant in the village
square. Cheap *menu du jour* with
seasonal dishes (such as asparagus)
and good local wines.

Le Bacchus Gourmand
Les Arcs-sur-Argens
Tel: 4 94 47 48 49
Fine Provençal cuisine and a wide
range of Côtes de Provence wines
available for tasting. Given the name,
this restaurant is appropriately
situated next to the headquarters
of the Comité Interprofessionnel
des Vins de Provence (on the N7).

Bruno
Lorgues
Tel: 4 94 73 92 19
Named after Clément Bruno, the
genial patron of the establishment.
Look out for the eye-catching mural
depicting him and his chefs as the
Apostles. The menu offers fine, rich
dishes, often with truffles.

Les Chênes Verts
Tourtour
Tel: 4 94 70 55 06
On the road to Villecroze this
restaurant has three small
interconnecting dining rooms.
The menu features refined dishes
with a classic touch, based on fresh
ingredients, such as truffles and
freshwater shrimps.

Le Colombier
Villecroze
Tel: 4 94 70 63 23
Serves quality Provençal cuisine
(*carré d'agneau à la fleur de thym,
marmite de St-Jacques aux blancs
de poireaux*). Stylish decoration;
outdoor terrace.

La Fontaine
Salernes
Tel: 4 94 70 64 51
A nice place for lunch, on a corner
overlooking the village square.
Market-fresh ingredients used in
dishes prepared with great care.

Le Gourmandin
Le Luc
Tel: 4 94 60 85 92
Two dining rooms here, serving
generous portions of well-prepared
seasonal dishes.

From Draguignan you can make an excursion to Figanières.
The D562 and D54 will take you to this picturesque little
village with its narrow, tortuous streets and covered
passages. The village is dominated by a church which rises
above the rooftops and is built on the site of a former castle.
Next door is the *Jardin des Senteurs*, a garden where some
150 different scented plants mingle deliciously.

Returning to Draguignan, next take the road to Les-
Arcs-en-Provence, past the magnificent Naturby waterfall.
Les Arcs has a medieval district known as the Quartier du
Parage, built on a steep hillside and best explored on foot as
parking is scarce. At the top is a ruined castle and fortifed
tower. From the terrace of the restaurant at the Logis du
Guetteur there is a fantastic view to be had of the
surrounding countryside. Head downhill again to Les Arcs,
then take a narrow road to the chapel of Ste-Roseline,
noted for its fine modern mosaic work by Marc Chagall.
Concerts and theatre performances are often staged
outdoors here at the chapel during the summer months.
Slightly out of town, on the N7 in the direction of
Vidauban, a visit to the *Maison des Vins des Côtes de Provence*
is recommended to obtain lots of regional wine
information, and there is a convenient restaurant next door.

Le Mas de Cotignac
Cotignac
Tel: 4 94 04 66 57
On the road to Carcès; this restaurant serves excellent food using regional ingredients.

L'Oustaou
Flayosc
Tel: 4 94 70 42 69
The good, inexpensive menu includes dishes such as *boeuf aux herbes*. Strictly Provençal cuisine. Overlooking one of the main squares in Flayosc, and always full for Sunday lunch.

La Petite Cave
Le Thoronet
Tel: 4 94 60 10 23
An unpretentious restaurant with country decor, a shady terrace and good traditional cuisine.

Le Relais des Moines
Les Arcs-sur-Argens
Tel: 4 94 47 40 93
On the road leading to the chapel of Ste-Roseline, this is a pleasant restaurant with friendly staff serving delicious food at reasonable prices. The vaulted dining room with a large fireplace is a feature of the place.

Le Tibouren
Carcès
Tel: 4 94 04 31 99
Named after the Provençal rosé grape variety, this is a wine bar doubling as an unpretentious restaurant, with many *grillades* on the menu. Also sells wine to take away.

LOCAL MARKETS

- Flassans-sur-Issole holds a market on Wednesday and Friday.
- Wednesday is market day in Besse-sur-Issole.
- Gonfaron holds its market on Thursday; Le Luc's is on Friday; Cabasse's is on Saturday, and Vidauban's is on Sunday and Wednesday.

Above The picturesque village of Cotignac is known for its glorious gardens filled with begonias, jasmine and geraniums, all of which flourish in the shelter of the 80-metre cliff face which towers above the village.

Below Once home to the Knights Templar, the Château d'Astros is now a renowned wine estate.
Below right Fountains abound in the sunbaked inland villages of Provence; this one is in Cotignac.

Fréjus and the Eastern Côtes de Provence

This route will take in all the eastern section of the Côtes de Provence appellation, including Fréjus itself, which is blessed with an excellent microclimate for winemaking. Wines here are said to have superior depth and structure to those made further west, and many are wood-aged, with potential for improvement in bottle. Most of the superior red wines include Syrah or Cabernet Sauvignon in a blend with old favourites such as Mourvèdre and Cinsaut, and they can be easily distinguished by the use of a Bordeaux-style bottle and presentation. More traditional Côtes de Provence wine, whatever the colour, still clings to the 'perfume bottle' format with elaborate labels and decoration. As a general rule, wines presented this way are rather nondescript, while bottles resembling the classics from other regions tend to have far more personality. The latter often have a specific domaine or château name on the label.

WATERFALLS AND WINES

Begin your journey in Les Arcs-sur-Argens and take the D91 past the chapel of Ste-Roseline. This winding road will eventually lead to La Motte, which had the distinction of being the first Provençal village to be liberated on 15th August 1944, by American parachutists. This event is commemorated by a monument near the golf course. There is an attractive old quarter of the village built on a wooded hillside with narrow streets and steep steps; the highest point is the Tour de l'Horloge, a rather weather-beaten clock tower which overlooks a square. Look out for the Moulin de Pizay and its distinctive vine mural; artist Robert Pizay exhibits his work here, including sculptures made from olive wood. For more energetic visitors, a board may

Left *The awe-inspiring Gorges du Blavet rising from the wooded landscape near Bagnols-en-Fôret.*

Above *One of several châteaux with d'Esclans in their name, all producers of good Côtes de Provence.*

Right *Puget-sur-Argens: the river is a vital source of irrigation for vines on the hot Provençal plains below.* Far right *Vineyards of the Alpes have to compete with dense forest.* Below *Vinous activities recorded on olive wood by artist Robert Pizay.*

FREJUS

RECOMMENDED PRODUCERS

LA MOTTE
Domaine de Clastron
Produces more red than rosé; the wines are spicy and go well with grilled dishes and barbecues.
Domaine du Jas d'Esclans
For rosé, red and white wines.
Domaine de St-Michel d'Esclans
This is the largest of the four d'Esclans *domaines* (and also the largest in the whole of La Motte). All its wines are generally good.

FREJUS
Domaine de Curebéasse
Mouth-watering, distinguished white wine, succulent rosé and magnificent red, including Roches Noires, aged in wood. The *domaine* is located near a roundabout on the road out of the town towards Bagnols-en-Forêt.

PUGET-SUR-ARGENS
Château de Cabran
Classy red wines are a feature here.

be found near the *mairie* mapping out five walks ranging from just over one to three hours. The Saut de Capelan, a 70-metre high waterfall tumbling from a vine-clad plateau, is well worth a visit. To get there by car, take the turning at the *monument aux morts* (war memorial) in the centre of the village, and follow the signs to Saut de Capelan.

There is another impressive waterfall, Pennafort, in a ravine north of La Motte; to get there, drive in the direction of Callas, past several wine estates with d'Esclans in their name. Not far from the waterfall is an eye-catching chapel with a round cupola, the ruins of an old tower and a pleasant hotel with restaurant. Track back south to the turning for Bagnols-en-Forêt. Halfway there the road starts to climb and twist as it approaches the Gorges du Blavet, a wooded ravine. The land becomes flatter again just before Bagnols-en-Forêt. The first building that you see is the isolated chapel of Notre-Dame-de-Pitié. To explore the village, park the car near the Place de la Mairie and climb the steps to the church, which is surrounded by chestnut trees. After being destroyed and abandoned at the end of the 14th century, the town of Bagnols was rebuilt in the 15th century by Italian families.

Continuing on towards Fréjus, traffic generally begins to increase and the outskirts of this town are rather bleak. Like almost all Provençal coastal towns, Fréjus suffers these days

Right *The Roman aqueduct at Fréjus was once 50 kilometres long and still has the power to impress.*

ROQUEBRUNE-SUR-ARGENS
Domaine de la Bouverie
Make excellent white Côtes de Provence, from casks (pure Rolle), sometimes also rosé and red. Also produce honey on the estate.
Domaine de Marchandise
Rosé is a speciality at this estate.
Domaine de Planes
Energetic, talented domaine producing a range of superior wines, among them the white Cuvée Elégance (a lot of Sémillon) and red wines made only from Mourvèdre or Syrah. Ask if you can taste the Muscat Sec (*vin de pays*). They also have rooms to let here, if the tasting gets too enthusiastic!

LE MUY
Château de Rouët
On the road to Bagnols, in a residential area. The rosé and red Cuvée de l'Estérel produced here have overtones of ripe blackberries; it also makes other delicious wines such as Cuvée Belle Poule.

GENERAL WINE INFORMATION
● Every year in August Fréjus celebrates the *Fête du Raisin*.

HOTELS

L'Aréna
139 Rue du Général de Gaulle
Fréjus
Tel: 4 94 17 09 40
Hotel with 20 rooms in a converted bank, close to the Place Agricola. Small, charming rooms, furnished in traditional Provençal style. Excellent restaurant; with fresh fish a speciality. Swimming pool. Friendly and welcoming.
Hostellerie les Gorges de Pennafort
Callas
Tel: 4 94 76 66 51
Between Callas and La Motte/Le Muy, near a ravine with a waterfall, this peaceful establishment has 16 comfortable rooms and is set in a large park, with a swimming pool. The food served in the first-floor restaurant ranges from good to excellent.
Les Résidences du Colombier
18 Rue Trémollet
Fréjus
Tel: 4 94 51 45 92
Holiday complex on the outskirts of Fréjus (in the direction of Bagnols). Sixty plainly furnished rooms grouped in small buildings, surrounded by pine trees. Large swimming pool. Average food in Le Rimaurescq restaurant.

from overdevelopment and high property prices. The town was founded by the Romans who named it Forum Julii and during the heyday of Roman occupation its population was much what it is today: about 40,000. On the west side of the town is the Arena, a gigantic amphitheatre (the oldest in France) which could hold over 10,000 spectators. North of the centre, in a quiet part of the town, are the ruins of some Roman walls, an open-air theatre enclosed by shrubbery, and a number of supports for the aqueduct which used to bring water to the town from a distance of more than 50 kilometres.

In the tenth century the powerful bishops of Fréjus built several impressive buildings, such as the Bishop's Palace and the Chapter House; the Baptistry was built by one of their predecessors in the fourth or fifth century. Next to the Baptistry is the Cathedral of St-Etienne which dates from 1200 and there is a museum in the adjoining cloisters which is a mine of information about the history of the area. Just outside the town, on the N7 in the direction of Cannes, is a pagoda built by the Vietnamese in memory of their compatriots who died in the First World War, while a little further along the same road is the chapel of Notre-Dame-de-Jérusalem, an octagonal building decorated by Jean Cocteau (he died in 1963 before it was finished). Continuing west on the N7 you will pass through Puget-sur-Argens, a town which is mainly a collection of new housing developments.

Much more attractive is Roquebrune-sur-Argens, reached via the D7. This 1,000-year-old settlement is a *village fleuri* (award-winning floral village) with a fine Gothic church and a number of attractive squares and arcades; ideal for a gentle stroll. Complete this circuit by driving back to Le Muy via the N7. Le Muy is not a glamorous place but away from the industrial area, the town centre still has the sights of the fortified Gothic church of Notre-Dame, and also a round tower which once formed part of the town's fortifications.

RESTAURANTS

La Cave Blanche
Place Calvin
Fréjus
Tel: 4 94 51 25 40
Restaurant in a cellar, a few steps
away from the cathedral. Delicious
fish dishes (such as *rougets au beurre
basilic*) are made by the female chef.

Les Pignatelles
La Motte
Tel: 4 94 70 25 70
Country inn (direction Bagnols)
where Provençal cuisine is served as
well as dishes from the south-west
(for instance *foie gras* and *cèpes*).

Les Potiers
135 Rue des Potiers
Fréjus
Tel: 4 94 51 33 74
Lamb, fresh fish and goats' cheese are
but a few of the ingredients used to
prepare some truly divine dishes. As
the name suggests, there is also a
pottery display. Near the Place Agricola.

LOCAL MARKETS

● Friday is market day in La Motte.
● Fréjus holds markets on
Wednesday and Saturday throughout
the year; also on Tuesday and Friday
from June to September inclusive.

Left *Cloisters in the medieval* Cité
Episcopale *(cathedral close) of Fréjus.*
Below *The romantically isolated
chapel of Notre Dame-la-Pitié at
Bagnols-en-Fôret.*

Cassis and Bandol

Not long ago, there were only four *appellations contrôlées* in Provence. Cassis was one, and its reputation is still founded on excellent quality white wine with plenty of body and depth. Beware of confusion with the French word for blackcurrants; Cassis the town has nothing to do with the syrup or the fruit.

Vines are cultivated on the walled, terraced slopes to the south of Cassis. They are fortunately shielded from the ravages of the *mistral* by the towering Cap Canaille cliff above. These terraces are known as *restanques;* vines cover some 200 hectares, a figure hard to believe considering the difficulty of cultivation here. However this is a favoured area for the vine with a warm microclimate (an average of 3,000 hours of sun a year) resulting in a robust, mouth-filling white wine. The 14 producers have to go to great lengths to ensure that the wines contain sufficient acidity by picking some of the grape varieties very early. Six grape varieties are allowed in white Cassis, including Ugni Blanc, Sauvignon Blanc, Marsanne and Clairette. The aroma of white Cassis is always more floral than fruity, although there are sometimes hints of ripe peach and dried fruit, as well as a hint of herbal pungency: myrtle and rosemary.

Sadly, the virtues of this agreeable white wine are overrated by the local merchants and prices are usually high. Its slightly salty tang is delicious with local treats such as top-quality anchovies and other seafood. Sipping it by the harbour front is a way of distracting attention from its cost.

CASSIS

'Whoever has seen Paris and not Cassis has seen nothing.' This is a quote from a Provençal poet, the aptly named Frédéric Mistral, about what was then a small harbour village. Cassis is on a bay, only 20 kilometres from Marseille;

Left *The vineyards of Domaines Bunan in Bandol, a substantial family business, founded in 1962.*

Above *A scene to inspire any amateur artist: colourful fishing boats in the harbour at Cassis.*

Above *One of the most photogenic vineyards in France; Clos Ste-Magdeleine, Cassis, on the terraced restanques of Cap Canaille.*

CASSIS

RECOMMENDED PRODUCERS

CASSIS

Château de Fontcreuse
The best white wine from this hillside château is the Cuvée Fontcreuse. It also makes a pleasant rosé, with peach aromas and a good balance.

Clos d'Albizzi
First-class white wine with a rich nutty aroma and delicate floral flavour, is produced at this estate, which dates back to 1523.

Mas de Boudard
Overshadowed by the Cap Canaille cliff, highest in Europe; its white wine is made in a weighty traditional style.

Clos Ste-Magdeleine
Spectacular terraced vineyards going right down to the sea. Delicious and aromatic white Cassis; the rosé made here is also worth trying. The owner, François Sack, collects old cars.

Clos Val Bruyère
Vineyards on the lovely *restanques* yield beautiful, floral white wine.

Domaine du Bagnol
Aromatic Blanc de Blancs. Try the rosé and the cask-aged red Marquis de Fesques, with its ripe aromas of redcurrant and cherries.

Domaine du Paternel
Successful, drinkable white wines.

because of its proximity to the city it is crowded at the weekends with overflowing car parks, so choose a quiet day in the week to look around. The old centre consists of 17th- and 18th-century houses, narrow streets and a few squares; one of the most beautiful buildings is the *hôtel de ville* which is surrounded by a park. It also houses the *Musée Municipal des Arts et des Traditions Populaires*, where exhibitions of contemporary paintings are usually organised during the summer.

The harbour at Cassis is a pleasing sight, lined with pleasure boats and a few remaining fishing boats, against an attractive motley assortment of pastel-coloured houses with colourful shutters. Cafés and restaurants along the quayside tempt strolling visitors in for a glass of pastis, a snack or a meal. Treat yourself to a sea excursion in an underwater observation vessel, or take a boat to visit the *calanques;* narrow, rocky inlets nearby. The most famous of these is at Port Miou, but the most beautiful is that of En-Vau, only accessible on foot, but worth the hour and a half of effort from Port Miou. To the south, Cassis is separated from Le Ciotat by the bulk of the Cap Canaille massif (416 metres high) which projects into the sea like a ship's prow. The Route des Crêtes runs above, across the mountain ridge; it is a tortuous road with many good viewpoints, but definitely not for those with a fear of heights. On one of the spurs of this massif, near the port, is a large 13th-century castle, built by one of the seigneurs of Baux.

Rosé wines from Cassis can be agreeable but the red wines from the area are generally considered indifferent. For good-quality reds it is better to drive along the coast a little and visit neighbouring Bandol.

Domaine des Quatre Vents
Attrractively located estate offering
a warm welcome. This white wine
is fragrant, pale in colour but with
a fine, long finish.
La Ferme Blanche
Blanc de Blancs, rosé, and red wines
from an old-established estate. The
red wine is interesting for its rich
mineral and vegetable bouquet.

GENERAL WINE INFORMATION

● A *Fête du Vin* is celebrated in
Cassis on the first Sunday of
September.
● Visit the Maison du Vin
(on the Marseille road) for tastings
and sales of a variety of local wines.

HOTELS

Le Clos des Arômes
Tel: 4 42 01 71 84
Small, charming hotel, near the town
centre. The 8 rooms are comfortable
and bright. Pleasantly furnished. Own
restaurant with Provençal dishes.
Les Jardins de Cassis
Tel: 4 42 01 84 85
With 36 rooms, this is the largest
hotel in Cassis, east of the town on
the D559. Most rooms have been
recently renovated. Of the 15 hotels
in Cassis, this is one of the few with
a swimming pool. It also has a garden,
but no restaurant.
Les Roches Blanches
Tel: 4 42 01 09 30
On the road to Port Miou, this hotel
is built on a rock overlooking the sea.
Rooms (26) with greatly varying
degrees of comfort and different
views. Beautiful swimming pool.
Fresh fish and *bouillabaisse* are the
restaurant's specialities. Half-board
terms are obligatory in season.

RESTAURANTS

Chez Vincent/Le Vieux Pavé
Tel: 4 42 01 35 19
Try the *gambas frites* (fried prawns)
or a salad with deep-fried mozzarella;
both are specialities of the house.
Nino
Tel: 4 42 01 74 32
An amusing harbour bistro which
serves Italian and Provençal dishes.
La Presqu'île
Port Miou
Tel: 4 42 01 03 77
The best restaurant in Cassis,
magnificent location. Contemporary,
regional cuisine. Shady terrace.

Top *Visiting the* calanques *near
Cassis by boat takes the tourist back
to the days before Provence became
a major holiday destination.*

Above *The town square at
Olliloules; an important centre for
flower production, not to mention
a wide range of fruit and vegetables.*

Bandol

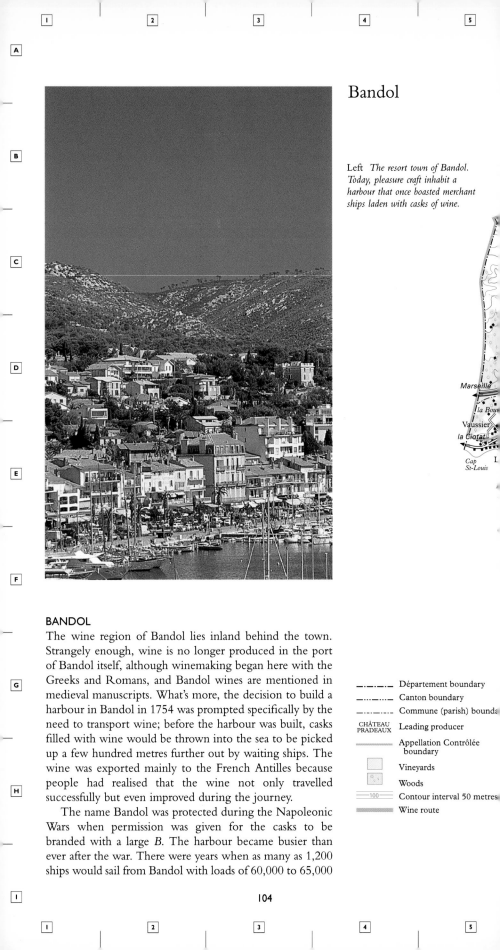

Left *The resort town of Bandol. Today, pleasure craft inhabit a harbour that once boasted merchant ships laden with casks of wine.*

Marseille
la Bou
Vaussier
la Ciotat
Cap
St-Louis

BANDOL

The wine region of Bandol lies inland behind the town. Strangely enough, wine is no longer produced in the port of Bandol itself, although winemaking began here with the Greeks and Romans, and Bandol wines are mentioned in medieval manuscripts. What's more, the decision to build a harbour in Bandol in 1754 was prompted specifically by the need to transport wine; before the harbour was built, casks filled with wine would be thrown into the sea to be picked up a few hundred metres further out by waiting ships. The wine was exported mainly to the French Antilles because people had realised that the wine not only travelled successfully but even improved during the journey.

The name Bandol was protected during the Napoleonic Wars when permission was given for the casks to be branded with a large B. The harbour became busier than ever after the war. There were years when as many as 1,200 ships would sail from Bandol with loads of 60,000 to 65,000

_._._._ Département boundary
_.._.._ Canton boundary
_.._._.._ Commune (parish) bounda
CHÂTEAU   Leading producer
PRADEAUX
~~~~~~~ Appellation Contrôlée
         boundary
⬜ Vineyards
⬜ Woods
══100══ Contour interval 50 metres
▨▨▨ Wine route

BANDOL

RECOMMENDED PRODUCERS

ST-CYR-SUR-MER

Château des Baumelles
An impressive building dating from the 13th century. Interesting red wine made here, with a rich, jammy nose and plenty of keeping potential.

Château Pradeaux
This historic château produces good red wines with plenty of wood age, which repay keeping for up to 15 years; and also an interesting rosé.

Domaine du Cagueloup
Fine white wine with a greenish tint and rich flavour made here; also a meaty rosé and liquorice-scented red made with Mourvèdre/Grenache.

Domaine de Frégate
Light white wine with grapefruit aromas, a delicate, salty rosé, and well-balanced peppery red. These wines are fairly light in style by the standards of this appellation.

STE-ANNE-DU-CASTELLET

Château de Castillon
The well-balanced rosé wine is recommended here.

Domaine de la Bastide Blanche
A few special wines, among them the red La Serre and an attractive rosé with a crisp lemon freshness.

LE CAMP-DU-CASTELLET

Domaine de la Bégude
Near the renowned motor racing track, this *domaine* produces a fine white wine with ripe fruit flavour.

LE BRULAT-DU-CASTELLET

Domaine de la Tour du Bon
A recently established *domaine* producing all three colours of wine which are equally drinkable.

LE CASTELLET

Château Romassan
One of the Ott family's properties with a strong emphasis on rosé; this wine is successful commercially and of high quality; it is labelled as Coeur de Grain. There is a smaller production of red Bandol labelled as Rouge Longue Garde and a white wine with a fine honeyed scent.

Domaine de l'Olivette
Attractive *bastide* with a *pigeonnier*. Delicate floral white wine and also produce a pale salmon-coloured rosé.

Domaine de la Vivonne
Top-quality red wines, wood-aged and tasting of black olives, from a high percentage of Mourvèdre grapes.

Right The Domaine de Souviou *has a long history in Bandol, for both vines and olives.*

casks on board. Bandol attracted many coopers who found plenty of work there; each year they would make a total of 80,000 *cayennes* (casks containing 200 litres). Barrels are still needed only for red Bandol wines – although white and rosé wines are also produced – because the red wine needs to mature in casks for at least 18 months, but nowadays there is only one cooper left in the region, at Ollioules.

Today you will see only pleasure boats in Bandol's harbour, and the winegrowers are based in the villages inland behind the town. The red wines from their cellars are relatively rich in tannin, with elegant firmness, an aroma of red and black berries and currants, spicy overtones and hints of aromatic wood. The main grape variety used here is the Mourvèdre, a black grape variety which thrives in Bandol's warm, dry microclimate. A minimum of 50 per cent Mourvèdre is obligatory for red Bandol, and after the obligatory barrel-ageing the wines benefit from further ageing in bottle, for several more years. Bandol reds have a peppery bite which goes well with all types of strong meat dishes, and unsurprisingly they are an excellent accompaniment to game.

The rosé wines of Bandol also have a spicy quality which marries well with local tomato-based dishes; the whites combine a tangy, aniseed-like aroma with plenty of fruit and freshness on the palate.

A CIRCUIT AROUND BANDOL

The wine route starts in St-Cyr-sur-Mer, which is reached via the Marseille-Toulon *autoroute*. St-Cyr is a typical holiday village, and the nearby Les Lecques beach is popular with tourists. On the Place de la Mairie here is a small replica of the Statue of Liberty, made by Bartholdi, the sculptor who designed the American original. A visit to the *Musée de Tauroecentum* on the coast road of Les Lecques is intriguing; it houses Greek and Roman artefacts including the body of a five-year-old child, dating from the fourth century.

To start a tour from St-Cyr-sur-Mer, first take the D86 to Ste-Anne-du-Castellet, one of the villages belonging to the *commune* of Le Castellet. Besides the various wine-growing *domaines* around the village, Ste-Anne also has a church dating from 1622. For a complete contrast, divert to see the Paul Ricard circuit, near Le Camp-du-Castellet, where car and motorbike races are held; there is also a car museum here.

The old fortified village of Le Castellet dominates the surrounding countryside from the top of a steep hill. It can only be visited on foot (pay to park on the edge of the village). The narrow streets are lined with shops, galleries, cafés and restaurants, all geared to suit tourists. The church of St-Sauveurin Le Castellet was built in the 11th century in a sober, Romanesque-Carolingian style. Behind and beside the church is a tenth-century castle, with the town hall occupying one of the wings.

LE BEAUSSET
Domaine de l'Hermitage
All its wines are of high quality, said to have flavours of spice, leather and pepper. The red wine ages well and the domaine also makes agreeable rosé and white wines.
Domaine Mazet de Cassan
On a picturesque road; noted for good rosé with an attractive orange tint, and for agreeable white wines.
Domaine de Souviou
An ancient estate growing both grapes and olives. Aromatic white, refreshing rosé and a red made from 75% Mourvèdre, with a pleasing bouquet of prunes and cherries.

STE-ANNE-D'EVENOS
Château Ste-Anne
A *domaine* dating back to the 16th century. Excellent wines made here.
La Laidière
One of the better producers, with elegant rosé and well-balanced red.

OLLIOULES
Domaine de Terrebrune
Not far from the Gorges d'Ollioules. Organises a first-class *table d'hôte* menu between June and Octoer when you can drink red Bandol (including old vintages). The wines here are said to taste strongly of *herbes de provence*.

LE PLAN-DU-CASTELLET
Domaine Ray-Jane
As well as the robust red wine and an aromatic rosé, this *domaine* has an interesting *Musée de la Tonnellerie* (including old cooper's tools and a wine vat over 250 years old).

LA CADIERE D'AZUR
Château de Pibarnon
Estate situated high on a hill, facing the sea, and rated one of the best Bandol estates for both red and rosé.
Château Salettes
The cellar is in an olive mill; the white wine is greenish in tint (like olive oil) and the red rich and fruity.
Château Vannières
The red wine is said to taste of truffles and prunes. The white Perle d'Azur and rosé Cuvée Spéciale are also recommended.
Coopérative La Cadièrenne
Not far from the *autoroute*, this cooperative is highly rated by visitors to the area. A bright pink rosé wine is produced here, with a delicious fruit-gum flavour.
Domaines Bunan
Historic family-owned business recently brought up to date with much improved wines as a result.

Château la Rouvière
One of several properties owned by Domaines Bunan. Reached via a narrow, winding road. Superior red, white and rosé wines. One of its labels is Moulin des Costes.

Domaine Lafran-Veyrolles
A small *domaine*, established for about 3 centuries. Extraordinarily successful wines. The red is made from 85% Mourvèdre, and they also make good quality white and rosé.

Domaine de la Noblesse
Classy wines with a powerful personality; the red wines need to be aged for some years in bottle.

Château Roche Redonne
The red is the most impressive wine, from this young estate; spicy and well-balanced in style.

Coopérative Moulin de la Roque
Good red wine produced here under their Sélection label.

GENERAL WINE INFORMATION

• There is a tasting room on the seafront at Bandol where you can taste the wines of the region.
• At the beginning of December Bandol celebrates the *Fête du Millésime des Vins de Bandol*.

HOTELS

Castel Ste-Anne
Ste-Anne-du-Castellet
Tel: 4 94 32 60 08
Pleasant hotel surrounded by a garden, with 17 rooms furnished in a contemporary style and a restaurant serving regional dishes. Also has a swimming pool.

Hostellerie Bérard
La Cadière d'Azur
Tel: 4 94 90 11 43
The 35 rooms are not large but they are very well fitted, with excellent bathrooms. There are also five suites., a terrace and a swimming pool. The restaurant looks magnificent and the food is superb. The Bérard family offer their guests first-class regional cuisine. You may safely leave the choice of wine to your hostess Danièle Bérard.

Hôtel de Frégate/ Le Mas des Vignes
St-Cyr-sur-Mer
Tel: 4 94 29 39 39
A paradise for golfers as this beautiful hotel complex (over 100 rooms, suites, villas) is near two golf courses, one with 18 and the other with 9 holes. There are also tennis courts and an enormous swimming pool. Riding is possible in the park. The restaurant is known for its innovative cuisine, and naturally serves wines from the Domaine de Frégate.

From here it is only a short ride to Le Beausset, a fair-sized village built around a 19th-century church. In front of the town hall is a pretty, triangular square with a small wine press. Continue on the N8 to Le Beausset-Le Vieux with its splendid view of Le Beausset and its surroundings. The Romanesque chapel built on a hill top has an interesting wooden statue of the Virgin Mary and attracts thousands of pilgrims on Easter Monday and Whit Sunday.

Follow the N8 further and, in Ste-Anne-d'Evenos, take the D462 to Evenos. A deep ravine and later a steep, winding road lead to the village. It nestles on top of the mountain like an eagle's nest and consists of a few houses and the ruins of a castle. From these walls there is a fantastic, panoramic view of the gorges of Ollioules.

Ollioules does produce wine, but it is much more famous for its flowers: it boasts France's largest flower market (Monday, Wednesday and Friday). In the centre of the village is a pretty little square, overlooked by the town hall and the 11th-century church of St-Laurent. From here, take the D11 to the fishing village of Sanary-sur-Mer and then the N559, which is a coastal road.

Bandol itself is geared to suit the tourist. Along the sea is a beautiful promenade lined with palm trees adjoining the pleasantly shady Place de la Liberté where a daily market is held. The town is a an ideal place to rest and relax in one of the excellent hotels. The Ile de Bendor is only a short boat trip away from Bandol. It is small and quite idyllic with

a Provençal village and a museum devoted to wine and spirits (bottles, glass, murals). Moving on from Bandol follow the road back towards Le Beausset, passing stalls selling flowers and wine. Look out for the turning leading to the famous winegrowing estates of Domaines Bunan, and then a *Jardin Exotique*, filled with plants and animals.

Continue on the D66 past Le Plan-du-Castellet towards La Cadière d'Azur, a 1,000-year-old village perched atop a hill. The medieval centre here still has the ancient fortified town gates, a narrow square on two levels, the chapel of Ste-Magdeleine (built on the foundations of a medieval castle) and the 16th-century church of St-André.

Complete the final stage of the Bandol tour by taking the D266 via La Madrague and Les Lecques back towards St-Cyr-sur-Mer. The Moulin de St-Côme makes a pleasant stop on the way. It is still a working mill where olive oil and many other regional products are on sale. To join the Côtes de Provence wine route again take the A57 from Bandol to Toulon and thence drive via the N97 to the town of Cuers.

Mas Lei Bancau
Le Beausset
Tel: 4 94 90 27 78
Peaceful hotel, owned by a Belgian couple, on the hill road leading to Le Beausset-Le Vieux. Some 8 rooms, most of them large, with shower or bath. Beautiful swimming pool and garden. No restaurant.

RESTAURANTS

Auberge de la Nonna
Le Beausset
Tel: 4 94 90 36 06
On the N8 in the direction of Toulon, this restaurant serves delicious, regional dishes with a smile. Ideal for those staying at the Mas Lei Bancau.

Auberge du Port
Bandol
Tel: 4 94 29 42 63
For years the best place in Bandol to go and enjoy *fruits de mer*, prepared in every possible way. Situated on the coastal boulevard, close to the market square.

L'Assiette Gourmande
Ollioules
Tel: 4 94 63 04 61
Good range of fish on the menu at this restaurant overlooking a small square by the church.

Castel Lumière
Le Castellet
Tel: 4 94 32 62 20
Reliable place to eat in the old village. Quite sophisticated Provençal cuisine.

Le Clocher
Bandol
Tel: 4 94 32 47 65
Small restaurant serving carefully prepared fresh fish dishes and seafood, near the market square.

La Fontaine des Saveurs
Le Beausset
Tel: 4 94 98 50 01
Modest rustic dining room. Delicious dishes made with fresh ingredients eg. *timbale de rougets sauce safranée*.

La Grange
Le Beausset
Tel: 4 94 90 40 22
Very popular locally, well known for its grills. Country ambiance.

Le Poivre d'Ane
Ste-Anne-d'Evenos
Tel: 4 94 90 37 88
Traditional fish, meat and game dishes. Also has a pleasant terrace.

LOCAL MARKETS

- St-Cyr-sur-Mer has a large market on Sunday, while La Madrague's is on Thursdays in July and August.
- Friday is market day in Le Beausset on Friday; Thursday and Saturday in Ollioules.
- Large market on Tuesday in Bandol.

Left *The Domaine de Frégate is not only a fine wine producer but also a 100-room holiday complex.*

Above *Vine cultivation in Bandol is not easy, the terraces demanding considerable manual labour.*

Toulon and the Southern Côtes de Provence

There is a valley on the north flank of the Massif des Maures where large quantities of Côtes de Provence are produced. The wines include red, white and rosé, much of which finds a ready market in the tourist bars and restaurants of the Côte d'Azur. The widest point of this valley is on a level with Toulon; it narrows towards Pignans, which is roughly 35 kilometres to the northeast.

Our journey through this valley starts in Cuers, a large village surrounded by modern housing developments. The centre of the village has retained some medieval aspects, such as remnants of the old town walls, and gates and houses dating from the 17th and 18th centuries. The church of St-Pierre is beautiful inside, with a splendid main altar made from various coloured marbles. From Cuers you can see a chapel built on top of a nearby hill, to mark the gratitude of the village for being spared during a cholera epidemic in 1878.

Puget-Ville, the next village, calls itself the *capitale du bon vin*. Several hundred families live partly if not entirely from winemaking, and belong to the local cooperative. An elegant statue of Diana, goddess of hunting, stands in the Place de la Liberté, which is slightly raised above street level in the centre of town, surrounded by narrow houses. Note the traditional *allée* of plane trees along the N97 leading north from Puget-Ville.

Carnoules was once the only train depot between Marseilles and Nice and often as many as 100 steam locomotives would be there at the same time; this period is commemorated by the locomotive installed next to the N97 road. The old village of Carnoules, dominated by the church, was built on the side of a hill. Note the bell tower

Left *Hyères was a fashionable 19th-century resort; it was more accessible from England than Nice or Cannes.*

Above *Eye-catching wrought ironwork for the church tower at Carnoules, once a major train depot.*

TOULON

RECOMMENDED PRODUCERS

CUERS
Château de Gairoird
Producer of good white wine.
Domaine de la Moutète
Established in a 200-year-old *bastide*, making lively white and rosé wines.

PUGET-VILLE
Château du Puget
Produces more red wine than rosé.
Coopérative
Makes pleasant, reasonably priced red Côtes de Provence wines which are marketed under various labels. It sometimes also calls itself Cellier St-Sidoine.
Domaine de Grandpré
Producers of a robust red Cuvée Spéciale. The owner collects old cars.

CARNOULES
Domaine du Grand Cros
The Canadian owner here makes delicious red and rosé wines.

PIGNANS
Château Barbeiranne
Ultramodern cellar in an 18th-century château with an emphasis on wood age. The rosé and white wines are critically acclaimed.
Domaine de Rimaurescq
Leading wine *domaine* set in an English-Provençal park. Produce excellent, concentrated red wine, plus delicious rosé and white.

PIERREFEU-DU-VAR
Château Montagne
Produces deep-coloured red Cuvée du Coseigneur; tannic and sturdy.
Château de la Tour de l'Evêque
Once the property of the bishop of Toulon, this estate has tastefully restored cellars with old presses, a beautiful fountain and pleasant wines, among them the red Cuvée Clos Caliguade. The Cuvée Pétale de Rose is a very light and delicate rosé.
Domaine de l'Aumérade
A 400-year-old wine estate with almost 1,000ha of vineyards. The *domaine* belongs to the Fabre-Cordier group. In 1994 the Fabre family commemorated the estate's 400th anniversary by opening a museum devoted to *santons* (figurines). Reliable wines made here are marketed under the names of various *domaines* and *cuvées*.
Domaine de Peigros
Makes an agreeable red wine for early drinking, rich in dried-fruit aromas.
Domaine St-Pierre-les-Baux
This estate is owned by the Kennel family, whose main business is cooperage.

with wrought iron work and a restored olive mill where exhibitions are held. Pignans, the northern point of the route, has a magnificent church with beautiful paintings, as well as several interesting wine *domaines*. In the Place des Ecoles is a statue of Jules Gérard who made a name for himself as a lion hunter in the last century. His house is now the town hall.

Take the D78 and then the D13 to Pierrefeu-du-Var via the valley of the Réal Martin. The present village was built below the old one but is still a few dozen metres above the floor of the valley. Near the car park on the edge of the village is a large terrace with a magnificent view. The eye-catching wing-shaped monument in grey stone commemorates the airship Dixmude which was based near here and lost in 1923. The church of St-Jacques-le-Majeur is being carefully restored. Continue on the D12 which will take you to the N98, not far from Hyères.

Left *View of Hyères from the Villa Noailles; a Cubist mansion designed by Mallet-Stevens in the 1920s and visited by all the Surrealist painters.*

RESTAURANTS

Le Lingousto
Cuers
Tel: 4 94 28 69 10
This is the best restaurant in the region. on the road to Pierrefeu. Located in a small bastide, it has quite large dining rooms and a romantic terrace surrounded by plane trees. Inventive, generous dishes with refined country overtones.

La Tuilière
Carnoules
Tel: 4 94 48 32 39
Good, affordable Provençal cuisine and friendly service may be found in this agreeable pink villa, on the N97 between Puget-Ville and Carnoules.

LOCAL ATTRACTIONS

● There is a flea market in Pierrefeu-du-Var every fourth Saturday of the month during the summer.
● Other markets occur in Cuers and Carnoules on Friday; Puget-Ville on Saturday and Pignans on Thursday.

HYERES

RECOMMENDED PRODUCERS

ILE DE PORQUEROLLES
Domaine de la Courtade
Impressive, expensive wines from a high-tech estate established in the 1980s. The red wine is made from Mourvèdre with a little Syrah. It is allowed to mature for a long time in cask and is unfiltered. The white has a grassy, floral bouquet and a scent of wood (after 9 months in barrique), like that of white Graves.

LA LONDE-LES-MAURES
Château du Galoupet
Facing the sea in a lovely setting rich in Mediterrranean flora. Makes some traditional, full-bodied and powerful white wine.

Château de Jasson
The rosé Cuvée Eléonore is a fragrant and complex wine.

Château Maravenne
The successful wines here include Fine Perle de Rosée (dewdrop) in its distinctively shaped bottle.

Château Ste-Marguerite
An excellent *domaine*; formidable red wine and a delicious white – M de Marguerite – plus superb rosé.

FROM HYERES TO ST-TROPEZ

The old health resort of Hyères is today a large town with elegant palm-fringed boulevards. The centre was built on the side of a hill dominated by the ruins of a large castle. A good place to start a walk through the town is the paved square in the Alphonse Denis gardens; note the unusual fountain with cranes spouting water, and next to it the statue of Charles I of Anjou, conqueror of Hyères in 1257. Next visit the Place de la République, with its 16th-century church of St-Paul and a picturesque pedestrian zone. For more details about the town's history go to the *Musée Municipal*, on the south side of the town. More intriguing is the Villa de Noailles, built in the mid-1920s, its style following the avant-garde, cubist style of the day.

There are regular crossings between the peninsula south of Hyères and the Ile de Porquerolles, a lovely car-free island where camp sites and smoking are forbidden. It is like

Clos Mireille
Home of an outstanding, striking (but pricy) white wine. Glorious coastal setting. Belongs to the Domaines Ott.

Domaine St-André-de-Figuère
New owner in 1992, since when the wines have been better than ever.

BORMES-LES-MIMOSAS
Domaine de l'Angueiron
Fine views of the port of Bormes and the coast. The white wine here is fresh and lemony; the red also good.

Domaine de la Malherbe
One of the best *domaines* of Côtes de Provence which used to be part of the presidential Fort de Brégançon. Red, white and rosé wines are made.

Domaine de Ste-Marie
The name of the *domaine* refers to a statue marking deliverance from a cholera epidemic in 1887. The light white Cuvée Spéciale made here is agreeable for early drinking.

Domaine de la Sanglière
On the road to the Château de Brégançon; the red wine is wood aged and has a velvety smoothness as a result, with ageing potential.

LA CROIX-VALMER
Domaine de la Croix
One of the first bottlers of Côtes de Provence.

RAMATUELLE
Château de Pampelonne
Successful red wine which is marketed by Les Maîtres-Vignerons de St-Tropez (see below).

Domaine des Tournels
Producers of the red Cuvée Rayne and other good wines.

GASSIN
Château Barbeyrolles
For good rosé, white and red wines.

Château Minuty
A reliable name. Try the special cuvées, notably the rosé, pale in colour but rich in exotic fruit flavour. The same family also runs the Domaine Farnet.

Les Maîtres-Vignerons de la Presqu'île de St-Tropez
Near the intersection of the N559 and the N98. Dynamic association of winegrowers producing some delicious wines; it is unusual for a cooperative to make its mark in this way. The best wines include the red Carte Noire, designed for long ageing, and the red wines of Château Farambert, Château de Pampelonne and Château St-Martin La Toche. An attractive shop sells wine and other Provençal specialities.

a large park with a wonderful range of fig trees, eucalyptus and other flora due to a mild microclimate, which is also ideal for grape growing. As a result, the island produces some eminent wines such as those of Domaine de la Courtade, one of three wine estates on the island. The island is also home to the *Conservatoire Botanique de Provence*, a paradise for plant lovers.

Once back on the peninsula, follow the signs for the N98 towards St-Tropez. The first village you come to is La Londe-les-Maures, which has several excellent wine *domaines*, not to mention a tropical bird park with a notable collection of toucans!

Continue on the N98 to Bormes-les-Mimosas, a beautifully preserved village built high on a hill; mimosas and flowering shrubs abound along its narrow streets, and it is home to many artists and craftsmen. Covered passages and steps lead to picturesque little squares, sometimes revealing unexpected panoramic views such as the one from the Place St-François-de-Paule. Bormes-les-Mimosas has its own museum of art and history. Above the village are the ruins of a 12th-century castle, and the Château de Brégançon, an official residence of the French president, is on the peninsula south of Bormes. The words *Les Mimosas* were officially added to the village name in 1968.

Above *The Domaine de Rimaurescq makes a highly rated, wood-aged red Côtes de Provence.* Left *Near-tropical conditions for these vines set amid palm trees at La Croix-Valmer.*

GENERAL WINE INFORMATION

● Taste hundreds of Côtes de Provence wines at the *Vignades*, which takes place in the open air in Hyères on the third Sunday of July.
● Wine festival in Ramatuelle on the first Sunday in July.

HOTELS

Bello Visto
Gassin
Tel: 4 94 56 17 30
On the panoramic terrace of the village. Has 9 rooms (7 with shower, two with bath). Not very spacious, but offers modern comfort. Also has a restaurant with a large terrace, serving Provençal cuisine.

La Vigne de Ramatuelle
Ramatuelle
Tel: 4 94 79 12 50
Relatively new establishment with a terrace overlooking a vineyard. All 13 suites have their own terrace and are very comfortable (air conditioning). It also has a large garden and a swimming pool with waterfall. Slightly outside the village, near the beaches.

RESTAURANTS

Au fil à la Pâte
Ramatuelle
Tel: 4 94 79 27 81
Small establishment offering fresh
pasta and some regional Provençal
dishes as specialities.

Le Jardin de Perlefleurs
Bormes-les-Mimosas
Tel: 4 94 64 99 23
Inspired Provençal cuisine, often of
impressive quality (*soupe de rouget au
bourride, crème brûlée* with a *confit* of
chestnuts). Also has an amazing wine
list with regional wines.

Lou Portaou
Bormes-les-Mimosas
Tel: 4 94 64 86 37
Country-style interior with a lot
of old paintings. Adequate cuisine,
decidedly traditional. Small terrace
in a covered passage.

L'Oustaou
Porquerolles
Tel: 4 94 58 30 13
Good for a relaxed lunch on the
market square (grills, pizzas, etc).
Also has a few hotel rooms.

La Petite Auberge de Barbigoua
La Croix Valmer
Tel: 4 94 54 21 82
The locals' secret restaurant, it is
situated on a hillside between
Cavalaire and La Croix-Valmer.
Delicious dishes prepared here
with market-fresh ingredients.

La Tonnelle des Délices
Bormes-les-Mimosas
Tel: 4 94 71 34 84
Between the car park and the old
village. A friendly restaurant offering
high quality Provençal cuisine. In the
morning, around 11 o'clock, hot *pain
de campagne* is usually served.

Continue along the winding coast road which runs between the Massif des Maures and the sea, with magnificent views across bays and capes. There are no vineyards to be seen until La Croix-Valmer, a typical sea resort with wide beaches. This was one of the places where the first landing craft of the liberation army landed in 1944. The village owes the first part of its name to the cross 100 metres high built on top of a hill in memory of the Roman emperor Constantine.

Leave the N559 and take the D93; the road climbs steeply with fine views of the landscape up to a plateau where boutiques, workshops, cafés and a dozen restaurants welcome you to the thriving tourist village of Ramatuelle. The church of Notre-Dame here dates from the 16th century and is part of the old fortified town walls.

Continue on to Gassin, a small village with just a few streets and remnants of the old fortified walls, but with a magnificent view. There are several restaurants here and an excellent art gallery. Take the steep road past the Château Minuty to the D98 which goes to Gogolin and Grimaud to the left, and on the right to St-Tropez.

LOCAL ATTRACTIONS

- Hyères has a garlic market around August 24.
- In February, Bormes-les-Mimosas organises a flower parade. At the end of April there is a cut-flower festival and at Whitsun, Bormes-les-Mimosas celebrates its fête.
- In July, there are music festivals at Bormes-les-Mimosas and Ramatuelle (jazz/classical music).
- La Croix-Valmer has a small museum devoted to regional flora and fauna, near the Cigaro beach.
- The painter André Quellier has a studio in Ramatuelle with an exhibition of paintings for sale.
- The village fête in Gassin takes place on or around August 10.

LOCAL MARKETS

- Daily market in Hyères on the Place de la République.
- Bormes-les-Mimosas holds a market on Wednesday and on Friday evening in the summer.
- La Croix-Valmer's market day is on Sunday.
- Ramatuelle holds a market on Thursday and Sunday.

Left The scenic town of Ramatuelle has attractive winding streets and arcades; it is also a centre for good Côtes de Provence wine production. Below A leisurely afternoon is often spent playing pétanque.

St-Tropez

RECOMMENDED PRODUCERS

COGOLIN
Château Garcinières
Faultless red, white and rosé Côtes de Provence is produced in this 12th-century castle, surrounded by shady trees. The best wines here are called Cuvée du Prieuré.
Château de St-Maur
This *domaine* is named after the patron saint of the village. It was one of the *domaines* awarded the *cru classé* during the 19th century.

GRIMAUD
Domaine de la Tourré
Traditionally made red wine recommended at this estate, which has been in the same family for 5 generations.

LA GARDE-FREINET
Château des Launes
The only local wine producer in this village; delicious wines are made including several styles of red.

GENERAL WINE INFORMATION

● *La Route du Rosé* is a sailing competition held under the name of the regional rosé wines. It takes place at the end of September.
● Grimaud organises a *fête des vignerons* at the end of August.

HOTELS

Athénopolis
Grimaud
Tel: 4 94 43 24 24
This hotel, built in 1990, has been given the old Greek name by which Grimaud was once known. The 11 rooms are tastefully decorated and equipped with every modern comfort. The hotel has an excellent swimming pool, but the shape may not appeal to everyone.
Hotel Mas Bellevue
St-Tropez
Tel: 4 94 97 07 21
A quietly located establishment (along the Route de Tahiti) that has about 40 comfortable rooms.

As the most famous beach resort in France, St-Tropez attracts a record numbers of visitors. From early spring to late autumn the little town is invaded daily by thousands of tourists. In the summer, especially at weekends and around lunchtime on weekdays, the town becomes completely overcrowded. All the camp sites are full to bursting and the town authorities find it difficult to keep all the amenities going and to ensure the place remains clean. The town owes a large part of its popularity to Brigitte Bardot and the other jetsetters who made St-Tropez a place where you go to see and be seen; above all the place is associated with glamour, wealth and a never-ending series of parties lasting well into the night.

That St-Tropez is the playground of the rich is apparent from the amazingly luxurious sailing boats and motor yachts moored in the harbour. In spite of all this, it is still a pleasure to visit St-Tropez; choose a weekday morning and park the

Right A windmill perched above the exquisite, and exclusive, medieval village of Grimaud.
Far right There is more to St-Tropez than its beach and harbour: the old town is well worth a visit.

Coq Hôtel
Cogolin
Tel: 4 94 54 63 14
Has 26 comfortable rooms
overlooking the village square.
Garden at the back where you can
also eat.

Hostellerie du Coteau Fleurie
Grimaud
Tel: 4 94 43 20 17
Pleasant rooms (14) in a hotel north
of the village centre. Ask for a room
with a view over the hills, or enjoy
the spectacle from the dining terrace.

 RESTAURANTS

Bistrot à Lices
Place des Lices
St-Tropez
Tel: 4 94 97 29 00
Excellent, creative cuisine served in
a *fin de siècle* atmosphere (or on
the terrace).

La Bretonnière
Grimaud
Tel: 4 94 43 25 26
Next to the Hostellerie Coteau
Fleurie; although the ambience is
rather sober the cooking is creative.

L'Echalotte
Rue Allard
St-Tropez
Tel: 4 94 54 83 26
Small establishment with one of the
best price-quality ratios in St-Tropez,
which is an expensive place.

Le Grille à Jeanine
La Garde-Freinet
Tel: 4 94 43 69 13
Pleasantly cluttered interior and, on
fine summer days, a terrace. Offers
nourishing country dishes, not only
Provençal but also Italian in origin:
osso buco, for example.

Le Lézard
La Garde-Freinet
Tel: 4 94 43 62 73
With a piano bar and jazz club.
Reasonably priced menu with a wide
choice (for instance, *lapin aux cèpes*).

Les Santons
Grimaud
Tel: 4 94 43 21 02
Restaurant with Provençal decor
preparing cuisine to a high standard.

car in the enormous car park in the *nouveau port*. At the
southern end of the *vieux port* is the *Musée de l'Annonciade*
which has a magnificent collection of paintings dating from
1890 to 1950, including works by Bonnard, Braque,
Matisse and Utrillo. The Rue Etienne Berny lies at right
angles to the old harbour. At number nine, you will find
the *Maison des Papillons*, which houses a collection of over
4,500 butterflies.

The narrow streets opposite the town hall lead to the church of Notre-Dame de l'Assomption, an 18th-century building with a wonderful pulpit by the sculptor Vian. Now try a visit to the citadel which dominates St-Tropez; its former dungeon is now a maritime museum with many exhibits relating to the town's glorious past. On the way back make a detour via Rue des Lices to go through the famous Place des Lices (now called Place Carnot), a square

Above *Many of the pleasure boats in the harbour at St-Tropez never leave their moorings; ostentatious entertaining takes place on board these private yachts in full view of the envious passers-by.*

LOCAL ATTRACTIONS

• St-Tropez celebrates Les Bravades in a spectacular way on May 16-18 with fancy dress parades and singing.
• Grimaud has a festival of classical dance which takes place in July and August.
• During the first weekend of October the *Nioulargue*, a large sailing event, takes place.
• There are 2 golf courses within the *commune* of Grimaud, Beauvallon (a 9-hole course) and La Vernatelle (a practice course); there is also an 18-hole course, Golf de Ste-Maxime, 10km from St-Tropez.

LOCAL MARKETS

• St-Tropez holds markets on Tuesday and Saturday (Place des Lices).
• Wednesday is market day in Cogolin.
• Grimaud holds a market on Thursday; La Garde-Freinet on Wednesday and Saturday.

with cafés and restaurants which tend to be crowded at lunchtime and in the evening. The most important wine producer in St-Tropez is the local *coopérative* in the Rue du Temple, near the Place des Lices.

To visit the local sights and vineyards, leave St-Tropez by the D98 and turn right at the roundabout for Port Grimaud, a modern-day Venice where every house is right on the water. The route leads on to Cogolin on the N8; this village produces a special kind of briar pipe, bamboo furniture, pottery, reeds for wind instruments, pewter artefacts and also carpets which are famous throughout the world, some of them adorning the Elysée Palace and the White House. Enthusiasts can admire them being made by hand at the factory: Manufacture des Tapis de Cogolin, Avenue Louis Blanc. You could also visit the Courrieu pipe factory which has a collection of 8,000 different models. The *Musée des Empreintes et Traditions Maures et Provence* is devoted to the history of the *département*. The old town centre of Cogolin has an almost medieval feel with its narrow streets and arcades. It stretches from the square in front of the town hall to the Tour de l'Horloge, the only remains of a castle which once stood on the hill. The church of St-Sauveur, near the *hôtel de ville,* dates from the 11th century but was rebuilt 500 years later.

From Cogolin it is not far to the artists' village of Grimaud, which is perched on top of a hill and dominated by the impressive ruins of a castle which is gradually being restored. Grimaud's centre consists of quiet little streets, small shady squares, well-maintained houses, a Gothic arcade and a Romanesque church with modern leaded windows; note the strikingly painted house opposite the church and the window boxes with flowers decorating many of the houses. The small chapel of St-Roch, in the direction of the cemetery, has beautiful frescoes and next door is a restored mill dating from the 12th century. The *Musée des Arts et Traditions Populaires* at Grimaud is open during the summer months, and the village always holds exhibitions during the tourist season.

The D558 which crosses the Massif des Maures is a pleasant road leading to La Garde-Freinet. Just before reaching the village, turn left and follow the signs leading to La Croix des Maures for fine views of the area. From the car park it is only a short distance to the ruins of a 15th-century castle. The Saracens also had a fort here high up in the hills as their last stronghold in this region, before they were finally driven out of France.

La Garde-Freinet itself is a typical Provençal village with some pretty squares, streets and fountains, a Renaissance church and also the small *Musée du Freinet* whose exhibits include objects found near the Saracen fort. A little further north of the village is the curious *Musée International de la Colombophilie* with every possible piece of information on the subject of homing pigeons, and about 1,200 of the birds themselves, housed in large cages.

Right Bougainvillea thrives in this idyllic climate – as here in Grimaud.

Nice and Bellet

The River Var concludes its course through Provence at Nice where it flows into the Mediterranean. The hills to the east of the Var Valley behind Nice are the birthplace of an almost secret wine: Bellet. As the vines grow some 300 metres above sea level they escape the worst of the summer heat below, and thus develop more finesse. Red, white and rosé Bellet wines are produced from regional grape varieties which include the red Braquet and Folle Noire, and the white Rolle. The reds are often aged in wood and have a fruity, aromatic fragrance combined with intense, powerful undertones. Some tasters claim to detect an almost Italian style which comes from the grape types used and the proximity to the border! The rosés can be most refreshing and elegant while the whites range from the gently aromatic to some with almost floral overtones. Chardonnay can be used in the blend to add quality and style. Because of its limited production with only 65 hectares of vineyards, most cultivated under labour-intensive circumstances, Bellet tends to be a relatively expensive wine. Most of the production is consumed on the spot in the restaurants of Nice.

There is a wine route right through the Bellet region; join it by taking the N202 from Nice or Cannes towards Digne. Turn off to St-Isidore then follow the signs to St-Roman-de-Bellet. The narrow road soon begins to twist as it climbs up into the hills. After five minutes or so there is a sign for the first wine *domaine*, Collet de Bovis/Domaine du Fogolar. A little further, observe the distinctive square tower of Château de Crémat; this belongs to the Bagnis family who, after the Second World War, were instrumental in saving the Bellet appellation from extinction.

Left *The heady scent of flowers fills the air at the elegantly sited main market in Nice.*

Above *The Negresco hotel in Nice features extravagant décor both inside and out; even the doormen dress up.*

In St-Roman-de-Bellet the best selection of these wines can be found in the grocer's shop behind the Auberge de Bellet. There are magnificent panoramic views over the valley of the Var and the surrounding hills from the church of St-Roman and other viewpoints along the road. Almost every square inch of the hills and plateaux is built on or used for the cultivation of various crops such as carnations (often in greenhouses) and there are no large areas where vineyards really predominate.

From St-Romain the road leads to Colomars, a village with the only hotel in the area. Just before the village, the wine route turns left, back to St-Isidore. The road winds on further past a few small producers and two large ones, Château de Bellet and Clot Dôu Baile.

Further inland, some 35 kilometres from St-Isidore (on the N202), is Villars-sur-Var. It is the only *commune* in the *département* of the Alpes-Maritimes which lies in the wine region of the Côtes de Provence. This is because of the efforts of a single excellent producer, Clos St-Joseph. The road leading to Villars-sur-Var is bordered on both sides by vineyards. The late-Gothic church of St-Jean-Baptiste (16th century) stands in the centre of the village and has beautiful sculptures and a splendid altarpiece; a gate next to the church leads to the Allée des Grimaldi, a double colonnade which was probably used in the past for training vines, pergola style.

On your way back to Nice it may be interesting to detour and see the Gorges de la Vésubie; turn off near Plan-du-Var, towards St-Jean-la-Rivière, then follow the road to Levens (high up in the ravine), and then on to St-Martin-du-Var. Vence and especially St-Paul-de-Vence, on the west side of the Vardal, are also decidedly worth a visit, not only for somewine tasting but also for their artists' colonies, famous galleries and superb luxury hotels and restaurants.

Below *In the Var Valley, almost every inch of available countryside is built on or used for cultivation.*

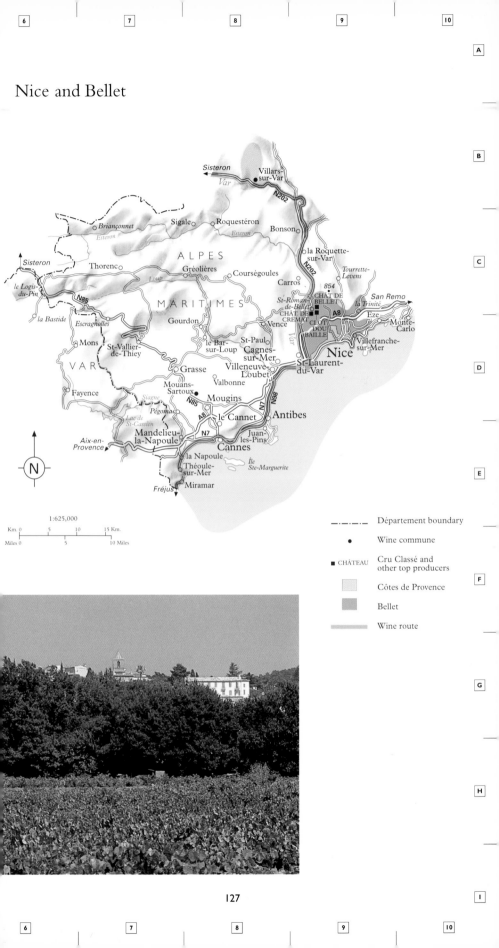

Nice and Bellet

NICE

RECOMMENDED PRODUCERS

NICE (QUARTIER DE CREMAT, BELLET-DE-NICE)

Collet de Bovis/ Domaine du Fogolar
This *domaine* belongs to university professor Jean Spizzo.

Château de Crémat
Largest producer with 11ha of vineyards. Good red wine with a rich meaty bouquet; also rosé and white Bellet. Looking at the castle you might think you were in Tuscany.

Propriété Massa
Traditional approach to winemaking is taken here, by one of the oldest wine families in the area.

ST-ROMAN-DE-BELLET

Château de Bellet
Leading producer of high-quality wines, and also one of the largest. Delicious, sophisticated wines; best are the white and the red Cuvée Baron G, named after Ghislain de Charnacé, the owner and one of the driving forces of the Bellet appellation.

Clot Dôu Baile
This estate makes wines with personality. The name means Clos 'of the head-shepherd'.

COLOMARS

Propriété Augier
Look for this estate opposite the Auberge de Bellet. Its wine label is rather whimsical, showing idealised locals in national costume.

VILLARS-SUR-VAR

Clos St-Joseph
Small estate (2.5ha) where excellent Côtes de Provence is made by the Sassi family. The red is supple and aromatic, with fragrant wood and vanilla overtones resulting from being aged in casks, and the oak-fermented, complex white wine is even classier.

Right *The Promenade des Anglais in Nice is now as much the domain of the car as the pedestrian.*

GENERAL WINE INFORMATION

● Fête de la Vigne, Nice on the first Sunday in September.

● The famous Chantecler restaurant at the Hotel Negresco in Nice serves a very rare white wine produced by the monastery on the Ile St-Honorat (off the coast opposite Nice). It is a *vin de pays* fermented in vats. About 1,000 bottles a year are produced. These monks also make a little red wine.

● St-Paul-de-Vence: serious efforts are being made to breathe new life into winegrowing here. The driving force behind this is Adrien Maeght of the Fondation Maeght art collection. At the moment a small amount of rosé is being produced.

HOTEL

Auberge du Rédier
Colomars
Tel: 4 93 37 94 37
There are 25 simple rooms, clean and spacious with adequate modern comforts. Those on the ground floor have a small terrace. Bellet wines feature on the restaurant list. Half-board is obligatory in season.

RESTAURANTS

L'Auberge de Bellet
St-Roman-de-Bellet
Tel: 4 93 37 83 84
Country restaurant, ivy-clad with a covered terrace and rather elegant interior. Regional dishes prepared with market-fresh ingredients.

Jean-François Issautier
St-Martin-du-Var
Tel: 4 93 08 10 65
Excellent restaurant on the N202, just outside St-Martin. Stylish decor and friendly, formally dressed waiters. Serves traditional dishes, adapted to the taste of today.

GLOSSARY

Aïoli – garlic mayonnaise

Allée – avenue

Appellation (d'Origine) Contrôlée (AC or AOC) – regulations which provide strict control of origin, alcoholic strength, quantity produced, grape varieties and methods used in French wine production. The exact nature of the AC varies from region to region, but the model for them all stems from the Rhône Valley, based on the legislation drawn up by the association of French *vignerons* led by Baron Pierre Le Roy de Boiseaumarie Armagnac

Atélier – work studio or artist or craftsman

Auberge – inn

Autoroute – the term used for a main motorway in France; most are *autoroutes à péage*, or toll roads

Banon – type of cheese made from goats' milk

Baoumo – ancient Provençal word for cave

Barrique – a barrel. In Bordeaux and Cognac, it refers specifically to an oak barrel holding 225 litres (or 300 bottles) of wine

Bastide – in Provence, a term for a country house. Historically, it meant a walled town in southwest France

Bauxite – a clay-like mineral containing alumina, the chief constituent of aluminium

Bouillabaisse – soup originally made by fishermen, containing fish boiled with herbs. The most 'authentic' bouillabaisse contains *racasse* and at least two other kinds of fish (including shellfish), and is coloured with saffron

Boules, or Jeu de boules – the game of bowls

Bourride – a Provençal fish soup or stew made from several kinds of firm, white fish. After boiling, the liquid is strained and bound with *aïoli* (see above)

Caillettes – meatballs or sausage made from minced pork, vegetables (often spinach) and herbs, served cold

Calanque – narrow, rocky inlet on the seashore

Carbonic maceration, or *macération carbonique* – A fermentation process used in making red wines in which fermentation takes place without the intervention of yeasts or even crushing the grapes. Whole bunches of grapes are put in a closed vat filled with carbon dioxide. Each grape ferments internally, a process which eventually explodes the grapes and yields mild, fruity wine designed for drinking young

Cave – can be used to refer to a cellar or to most any wine establishment

Cave coopérative – a cooperative winery run by and for wine-growers

Cayenne – cask containing 200 litres

Cépage améliorateur – literally, 'vine improver'; Syrah is used as this to upgrade otherwise ordinary Provençal wines by giving them the potential to age

Cèpe – an edible and highly regarded boletus mushroom

Chambres d'hôte – literally, 'rooms of the host': rooms let to tourists by private citizens, similar to a B&B in the UK

Château – while the word literally means a castle or large house, in wine terms it refers to any wine estate, regardless of size

Chènevrières – hemp fields

Choucroute – French for sauerkraut

Clos – a term of some prestige, used mainly for distinct, often walled vineyards sometimes in single ownership

Commune – refers either to a town or village, or to the area that surrounds the town or village – ie a district or parish

Comté – a count or earl, or earldom

Coquillages – shellfish; *coquille* means 'shell'

Côte – literally means 'hillside', but in wine terms it refers generally to a particular vineyard that is considered far superior to vineyards on surrounding plains. When used in names of *appellations contrôlées* (Côte-Rôtie, etc) it means the same thing

Coteaux – means the same as *côte* (see above)

Cours – promenade or walk

Cru classé – literally means 'classed growth'. Cru is a specialist term for a vineyard, usually one of high quality. A cru classé, then, is a vineyard (or the wines therefrom) that has been classified as being of a superior quality

Cuvée – refers to wine contained in a *cuve*, or vat. In certain wine regions – eg Champagne – the term is synonymous with 'first pressing'; elsewhere it is used simply to refer to 'blend'. Often, though, it merely refers to one 'lot' or 'batch' of wine, and can be used to mean a bottled wine

Daube – a traditional country beef stew. The word alone also means a joint of beef braised in wine

Département – a territorial division which refers to one of the 95 main administrative divisions or regions of France

Domaine – similar in meaning to *château*, but more usually refers to the property or estate, not the 'house' itself

Foire – a fair; often used the same way as *marché* or fête

Fruits de mer – seafood

Gambas – Mediterranean prawns

Gîte – self-catering cottage or flat

Gîte rural – self-catering house or cottage in the country

Grillade – term for food that has been grilled or broiled; especially meat

Hectare (ha) – a measure of area, usually considered to be 2.47 acres

Hôtel de ville – town hall

Herbes de provence – a mixture of basil, thyme, rosemary, bay, and savoury

Mairie – another name for town hall

Marc – grape-skins left over after pressing. Also the strong-smelling brandy that is produced from them, similar to Italian Grappa

Marché – market

Mas – term for a manor house, estate or farm in the South of France

Massif – a compact group of mountain heights

Microclimate – a term referring to the climate within a defined, usually restricted, space or position, including the spaces between the rows of vines. More usually, however, it refers to the climate of the entire vineyard canopy

Mistral – the cold, northerly wind that blows down the Rhône Valley and southern France before heading out into the Mediterranean. Although it produces headaches among many people subjected to it, it also helps to keep vineyards disease free

Oidium – French name for powdery mildew, a disease which afflicts vines

Oratoire – an oratory, or small chapel

Osso buco – country dish of Italian origin whose name means 'bone with a hole'. It consists of a stew of unboned veal knuckle braised in white wine, with onion and tomatoes, and is usually served with pasta or rice.

Pastis – an aniseed flavoured, usually high-strength, alcoholic beverage popular in the South of France, similar to Pernod. The name literally means 'confused' or 'mixed', which reflects the drink's cloudy nature

Pétanque – a type of bowls played in the South of France

Phylloxera vestatrix – a small, yellow, aphid or 'vine louse' which feeds on the roots of grapevines and has a more devastating impact on viticulture than any other pest or disease

Pieds et paquets – dish made from lamb belly and pigs' trotters

Pissaladière – a pizza-like, flat onion tart with black olives and anchovy fillets

Plat du jour – dish of the day

Racasse – scorpion fish

Ratatouille – a mixture of aubergines, peppers, courgettes, tomatoes and other vegetables, cut into cubes and braised in olive oli and garlic

Rouget – red mullet

Rouille – spicy garlic Provençal sauce that is a traditional accompaniment for *bouillabaisse*. The name - meaning 'rust' – describes its colour, which comes from red chillies and (sometimes) saffron

Route nationale – main or secondary motorway

St-Pierre – a type of fish

Santon – an ornamental figure at a Christmas crib

Schist – metamorphic rock composed of laminated, often flaky parallel layers

Seigneur – historical term for a lord or overlord

Seigneurie – domain belonging to a *seigneur*

Tapenade – a Provençal condiment made from capers, desalted anchovies and stoned black olives, all of which are pounded together in a mortar and seasoned with olive oil and lemon juice. It accompanies crudités or can be spread on slices of toast

Terroir – a problematic term that has no precise cognate in English. In general, it refers to the general physical environment of a vineyard, including the soil and all its layers, how it relates and reacts to the local climate and microclimate and how it ultimately influences the wine. Thus a wine from a specific vineyard will exhibit influences of *terroir* that are unique to that vineyard

Tire-bouchon – a corkscrew

Tomme de Banjols – a fresh goats' cheese

Tour de l'horloge – clock tower

Troubadour – a medieval French lyric poet of the 11th-13th centuries

Vendange – harvest

Village fleuri – award-winning floral village

Vin délimité de qualité supérieure (VDQS) – French quality designation that falls between *appellation contrôlée* and *vin de pays*

Vin de pays – freely translated, 'country wine'. The term as a category came into use in 1973, and refers to from specific origins, such as a particular village or an entire region or département, such as *Vin de Pays du Gard*. There are more than 140 *vin de pays* names currently in use, and they fall into three categories: regional, departmental and something called *Vin de Pays de Zone*, which is the most precise classification

GAZETTEER

INDEX

INDEX

INDEX